Language and co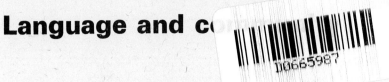

Explorations in Language Study
General Editors
Peter Doughty   Geoffrey Thornton

LANGUAGE AND COMMUNITY

Anne and Peter Doughty

EDWARD ARNOLD

© Anne and Peter Doughty 1974

First published 1974
by Edward Arnold (Publishers) Ltd
25 Hill Street, London W1X 8LL

ISBN: 0 7131 1854 7

Already published in this series

Language in the Junior School
E. Ashworth

Language Study, the Teacher and the Learner
P. S. Doughty and G. M. Thornton

Language, Brain and Interactive Processes
R. S. Gurney

Explorations in the Functions of Language
M. A. K. Halliday

Learning How to Mean: Explorations in the Development of Language
M. A. K. Halliday

English as a Second and Foreign Language
B. Harrison

Language in Bilingual Communities
D. Sharp

Language, Experience and School
G. M. Thornton

Printed in Great Britain by Butler & Tanner Limited
Frome and London

General introduction

In the course of our efforts to develop a linguistic focus for work in English language, now published as *Language in Use*, we came to realize the extent of the growing interest in what we would call a linguistic approach to language. Lecturers in Colleges and Departments of Education see the relevance of such an approach in the education of teachers. Many teachers in schools and in colleges of Further Education see themselves that 'Educational failure is primarily *linguistic* failure', and have turned to Linguistic Science for some kind of exploration and practical guidance. Many of those now exploring the problems of relationships, community or society, from a sociological or psychological point of view wish to make use of a linguistic approach to the language in so far as it is relevant to these problems.

We were conscious of the wide divergence between the aims of the linguist, primarily interested in language as a system for organizing 'meanings', and the needs of those who now wanted to gain access to the insights that resulted from that interest. In particular, we were aware of the wide gap that separated the literature of academic Linguistics from the majority of those who wished to find out what Linguistic Science might have to say about language and the use of language.

Out of this experience emerged our own view of that much-used term, 'Language Study', developed initially in the chapters of *Exploring Language*, and now given expression in this series. Language Study is not a subject, but a process, which is why the series is to be called *Explorations in Language Study*. Each exploration is focused upon a meeting point between the insights of Linguistic Science, often in conjunction with other social sciences, and the linguistic questions raised by the study of a particular aspect of individual behaviour or human society.

Initially, the volumes in the series have a particular relevance to the role of language in teaching and learning. The editors intend that they should make a basic contribution to the literature of Language Study, doing justice equally to the findings of the academic disciplines involved and the practical needs of those who now want to take a linguistic view of their own particular problems of language and the use of language.

Peter Doughty
Geoffrey Thornton

Contents

To the Reader

For all those teachers who are willing to go
beyond their own classrooms to seek answers
and particularly for the teachers in Northern
Ireland who asked us to write it all down.

Language and Community is not a research monograph, it is not a
'survey of the literature', it is not a contribution to any one
academic discipline, it is a book which sets out to tell a story,
a story about man's most distinctive attributes, his culture,
the environment which he makes for himself, and his language,
the means by which he makes this environment meaningful. We
say 'a story', because we ask the reader to begin at the beginning
and treat it as he would a continuous narrative, reading on to
discover what comes next, and how this may modify his view of
what has gone before, allowing each episode to add its own contribution on the way, though its full significance may only appear
at the end. We call it a story, because we ask the reader to participate in the action by bringing to the narrative at each stage
his own cumulative experience as a human being who has learnt
successfully to use language in the context of one, or many,
particular communities. We want the reader to test what we say
against the record of his own intuitive knowledge of how language
and community interrelate in the lives of all of us.

What, then, does this story have to say about something as
familiar and commonplace as our experience of using language and
living in communities? Our first step is to persuade the reader to
see that language is not 'out there', like a constructional toy given
to us in appropriate instalments as we grow from infancy to
adulthood, but an intimate part of each one of us. Language is
not like a *commodity* we own, but the outcome of a process of
growth and development, growth and development that involves
the individual child in a continuous interaction with the people
and objects of his world. In learning our language, we do not
simply 'take over' passively the 'elements and structure' of our
mother tongue as they are presented to us in the speech of those

9

around us. We are active participants in the language learning process, because it is essentially a process by which we strive to make the world meaningful to us. M. A. K. Halliday gives a brilliant analysis of this complex process in his volume in this series, called *Learning How to Mean*.

Language, for us, as human beings, however, implies a human environment in which we use our language, and thus the next step is to look at this environment as the context in which the infant learns how to become a *social* being, that is, learn how to make relationships with others and find out what those relationships mean. We use the word 'community' for this specifically human environment of relationships which provides the necessary habitat for man as a social animal. It is through his interaction with others, however, that the child learns language, and thus our use of the word 'community' necessarily refers also to the environment for the specifically human activity of using language. This intimate inter-relationship between the community the child inhabits and the language he learns leads us on to consider how the language we learn shapes so positively the meanings we give to what we experience of the world.

Our story then goes on to consider how the school stands in relation to this intimate interconnection between the language we use and the community we inhabit, and a consideration of school in relation to community raises the question of how human beings accommodate to change. 'Going to school', we would argue, is one of the most fundamental changes the ordinary human being has to face in the normal course of his life, because it is the first time most of us are asked to step out of our own familiar community and into another. A critical feature of this change is that school is not just a new and unfamiliar place, where the child has to learn new ways of behaving, but a new and unfamiliar *language climate*, where he has to learn new ways of using language, and a new medium, writing. In order to understand what we demand of pupils when we ask them to use language as the school requires, we need to see how great a contrast there is between our habitual ways of learning and using language, as members of family and community, and the ways customary in formal education. This brings our story to the point where the next step is to focus upon 'the language climate of schools' and that is where the book ends, for 'the language climate of schools', as we suggest in our postscript, requires a book to itself.

What we hope the reader will gain by following our story to this point is the realization that there is more to the matter of pupils using language to learn than a consideration of what is done in class-rooms. Pupils are individual human beings who have learnt language in the process of learning how to live the life of their communities: the whole process has taken place in the context of the patterns of relationships, habits and values that make up that specifically human environment. If we are to make sense of the pupil's problems and needs when he comes to use the language he has learnt in the context of the school, then we must be very clear about the processes by which he has learnt it, and the human environment in which the learning has taken place.

It remains only for me to do two things: make one brief comment on a linguistic problem of co-authorship, and acknowledge the help we have had in the writing of this book. Co-authors work in many different ways, but we choose to have one of us write the text, while the other acts as stimulus, commentator, critic and devil's advocate. In this case, Anne Doughty wrote the text, while I filled the other available role—hence she is the 'I' of the text. 'We' refers on some occasions to 'both of us' and on other occasions to 'all of us', that is, as human beings, for the reader and his experience is included in much of what we have to say. This difference, we hope, is clearly defined by the context. In this way we have tried to avoid such cumbersome locutions as 'one of the authors' 'my co-author' and so on.

A book of this kind grows out of a cumulative experience of reading and talking over many years. We wish to thank all those teachers we have met in our work together presenting *Language in Use* to audiences up and down the country, audiences whose comments have been so valuable a stimulus to thinking and so rich a source of illustration and representative example. We would also thank the students of Manchester College of Education for all they have let us hear of their personal experiences, experiences which throw so strong a light upon the central theme of this book. Finally, we would like to thank Sister Anne McCarrick and Patricia Bertenshaw, both practising teachers in Northern Ireland, and Janet Ede, our friend from Matlock College of Education, for giving their time and energy to reading our early drafts and commenting so usefully upon them. Their help and encouragement was a critical factor in the finishing of this book.

Peter Doughty

Manchester 1973

1 Language

1. Language is learnt from others

When a human infant is born into any community in any part of
the world it has two things in common with any other infant,
provided neither of them has been damaged in any way either
before or during birth. Firstly, and most obviously, new born
children are completely helpless. Apart from a powerful capacity
to draw attention to their helplessness by using sound there is
nothing the new born child can do to ensure his own survival.
Without care from some other human being or beings, be it
mother, grandmother, sister, nurse or human group, a child is
very unlikely to survive. This helplessness of human infants is in
marked contrast with the capacity of many new born animals to
get to their feet within minutes of birth and to run with the herd
within a few hours. Although young animals are certainly at
risk, sometimes for weeks or even months after birth, compared
with the human infant they very quickly develop the capacity to
fend for themselves. It would seem that this long period of vulner-
ability is the price that the human species has to pay for the very
long learning period which fits man for survival as a species.

It is during this very long period in which the human infant is
totally dependent on others that it reveals the second feature
which it shares with all other undamaged human infants, a
capacity to learn language. For this reason, biologists now suggest
that language is 'species specific' to the human race, that is to say,
they consider the human infant to be genetically programmed in
such a way that it can acquire language. This suggestion implies
that just as human beings are designed to see three-dimensionally
and in colour, and just as they are designed to stand upright
rather than to move on all fours, so they are designed to learn and

use language as part of their normal development as well-formed human beings.

Before we proceed we must look at the terms 'well-formed' and 'undamaged' as they have been used in the last paragraphs. There are many human beings who do *not* learn language despite the fact, that, like all other human beings, they are genetically programmed to do so. The reasons for this failure are very varied. At one end of the range there are individuals who havé suffered brain damage; at the other, individuals who have suffered severe emotional or psychological damage or deprivation; and in between these two, those who possess physical defects like misshapen articulatory or respiratory organs or total deafness. Any one of these handicaps, or a combination of them, will make language learning difficult, or impossible, for these individuals and therefore what is said in this book cannot be applied to them without a modification appropriate to their condition. When we speak of a 'normal' human being, therefore, we mean no more than one who is not handicapped in ways such as these. This does not mean that the ordinary undamaged individual may not have difficulties, even extreme difficulties, to overcome in order to learn language, but it does mean that these 'difficulties' arise out of the ordinary business of living and do not derive from physical or mental handicaps.

Even if we consider a normal infant genetically programmed to learn language, there is still a further condition that has to be fulfilled before language learning can take place. The infant must be born into a properly constituted human environment. In other words, he must spend the period of physical dependence upon others in an environment where there are adults using language in the course of their day to day life and in the course of their care of the child. The importance of this human environment is critical to the child because the capacity he has to use language is a *capacity* only. In order to *realise* this capacity by the acquisition of the patterns of a natural language he must become part of a language-using group so that there is the substance of a language in use for his capacity to work upon.

An example may help to illustrate this key point in our argument. Most readers of this book can be supposed to possess a latent physical capacity which they could use if they wished to learn how to swim or how to play a musical instrument, but it is highly likely that some readers do not in fact swim, or play a musical instrument, because at a critical point in their develop-

14

ment they either did not have access to swimming pools or musical instruments, or they did not feel any particular desire to engage in these activities. The presence of an appropriate context, both physical and cultural, is a key factor in realising human capacity. It may well be that the readers who have not realised their capacity to swim or to play a musical instrument are those who grew up in the years before swimming pools became a feature of most towns and playing musical instruments became a fairly normal part of the activities of schools.

Now, just as it is easier for a potential swimmer to realise his capacity in a town with a swimming pool, swimming clubs and an active interest in swimming, so there are some human contexts which actively encourage language learning while there are others that may severely inhibit the process. The inhibiting capacity of many human contexts is a major theme of this book to be taken up in the later chapters. What must be said here is that for a human being to realise his capacity to language, not only must he be physically undamaged, but also he must have a proper human context in which to exercise his capacity. This context is provided by the human group into which he is born and the community of which that human group is a part.

As far as the child is concerned it is immaterial whether the language used by that community is English or French or Swahili, or whether there is one, or more than one, language being spoken within it. His capacity is a general capacity and can be used on whatever language or languages his community presents to him. A particularly clear example of this general capacity is the fact that all well-formed infants are physically capable of making any of the sounds used by any of the world's natural languages. Indeed, at an early stage in his development, the infant 'practises' a whole range of sounds in the process of focusing upon those that are used by the adults who surround him. Later, however, the sounds that he does not hear spoken in his own environment are 'forgotten' as he comes to master the sound patterns of the language he is learning.

One way of approaching this question of the child's general capacity to learn language is to look, not at what happens in a 'normal' situation, but instead at what can happen in a situation where the child does possess his normal human capacity to learn language, but is *not* given the necessary context of human language activity in which this capacity can be realized. Such situations, where a child is deprived totally of a proper human environment

15

are few but they are now known to exist. In very many countries we have, preserved in myth and legend, accounts of children reared by animals. At the same time, we now have, in addition, authenticated accounts from the nineteenth and twentieth centuries of so-called 'feral' children, that is, children who have spent their formative years growing up in a non-human environment. We can reconstruct something of what must happen in these cases. In the first place, if a child is cared for by an animal it will be in contact with that animal and with other animals in the flock or herd or pack. The sounds and movements, tastes and smells of this animal world are in no way 'strange' to the child, for every child is born into an equally unknown world, whether its home is a high-rise flat in England, a peasant cabin in Central Spain, a long house in Borneo or a wolf's den. No matter where a child is born, it is surrounded by unknowns. The fact that part of the process of learning to be human requires a child to make sense of these unknowns has lead at least one American psychologist, George Kelly, to suggest that 'Man is a problem-solving animal'. This would certainly help to explain how incredibly rapidly human infants learn to make sense of their different environments and to use the patterns of language they discover within them. Kelly's suggestion also helps us to see how a human infant could survive in the context of a wolf-pack by learning rapidly what was required of him as a wolf. We can illustrate this by looking at what would be likely to happen to his general capacity to language, were he to find himself in this non-human environment. He would apply this general capacity to the sounds of the pack which surround him and which do have meaning in that context. He learns to make and use the sounds of the pack just as he would were he working with the speech sounds of a human environment. Just as every child on the road where this book is being written knows the meaning of four off-key notes used by the local ice-cream man to signal his arrival, so the feral child will learn very quickly the meaning of such sounds as danger calls. He will also have the capacity to make these calls when he has learnt both how to make the appropriate sound and how to recognise the appropriate context in which the sound will have meaning. What is happening is that the human child is using his general capacity to acquire language, and to 'problem-solve', but he is using them in a *non-human* environment. What this means, ultimately, is that the human child cannot in fact become fully human, because he has not had a human environment from which to learn the language and behaviours which distinguish human beings from animals. The feral child cannot, because of his situation, become an effective human being, but he can in many senses become a very good wolf!

By focusing on this abnormal situation we have tried to show what we mean when we say that a child is born with a general capacity to acquire language. The environment in which that capacity is able to operate will vary enormously from child to child, but the capacity itself has well-defined characteristics which do not vary. No two human beings are exactly the same, even monozygotic twins, but for every well-formed human being we can quote a list of necessary features; one head, two arms, two legs, two eyes, one nose, one mouth, two ears and so on. There is, in fact, a basic design for human beings carried by the genetic programme for the species. Locally, in response to certain conditions, individual features of the design may be modified. For example, Andean Indians living at high altitudes have a much larger chest capacity than Chileans living at sea-level; some desert dwelling peoples have a thick epicarthic fold over the eyes which acts like a built-in sunshield; some desert-dwelling tribes also have the capacity to store fat in the buttocks, but nevertheless we accept that all human beings have chests, eyebrows and buttocks. Similarly, every child is born with the capacity to learn language and to use the language so acquired in order to make sense of the world into which it is born. How it does this, and with what success, and in what environment, are subject to variation and modification. What is *not* open to modification in a well-formed human being is the actual capacity to do both these things; to learn language and to make sense of the world.

2. Language is not just 'words'

In the last section we suggested that a human infant is genetically equipped to learn language providing that it is not handicapped in any way, either by damage or physical deformity or by extreme deprivation in terms of its experience of a human environment. We were making the fundamental, if obvious, point that language can only be learnt through the child's involvement in an environment where adults are using language in the course of their everyday life. To hear language spoken in the environment is certainly an essential for the developing child, but language is more than words and sounds, it is also *meanings*. Hearing language spoken, of itself, however, is not going to give the child the opportunity either to make meanings or to acquire language.

Let us look at one brief instance of a child learning how meanings and words go together. Some months ago I was visited by an eighteen-month-old girl and her mother. I offered the little girl some orange juice and while her mother used the telephone I suggested that she come with me to the kitchen to fetch it. The little girl began to follow me, but on the way she stopped short at a waste paper basket containing among other things the previous day's newspaper. This she carefully picked out and spread over a large area of carpet. When satisfied with her work she sat down in the middle of the papered area and said with a questioning tone 'Orange juice?'. I was so interested in what she was doing that I had forgotten all about the orange juice. At this point Victoria's mother explained to me that as they had moved into a new house with new carpets six months after Victoria was born, spreading a newspaper was a standard procedure before orange juice. For Victoria, 'orange juice', 'drink' and 'newspaper' were all known elements in a situation which had occurred many, many times even in her brief eighteen months' experience of living. She had learnt not only to make the sounds which others would identify as 'orange juice' but she had learnt also that these sounds signified the drink she wished for, and, more than that, by pronouncing them she could cause others to produce the drink. Victoria had learnt two crucial things; that objects have names and that the correct saying of a name is a form of action. She had both seen and touched and drunk 'orange juice' and discovered that these sounds would produce the drink. In other words, her learning what those words mean was a function of experience, involving the active deployment of the words themselves and her accurate observation of their effects upon others. In addition to this, Victoria had learnt implicitly an important piece of information about the behaviour of people in her community. Her mother's insistence on spreading a newspaper before eating or drinking had made available to her in a concrete form the abstract idea of 'cleanliness' without there being any need for her to meet the abstract noun itself.

It would be quite splendid if at this point we could devise a situation in which the reader divested himself of the enormous experience he has of making sense of the world, so that he could see how it is that a human infant has to be involved in *using* the language he experiences in the course of daily life if he is to 'make

18

meanings' successfully out of what he hears about him. We cannot do this, of course, but what we can do is ask the reader to imagine situations in which he, as an experienced adult, might well have difficulty in using language. This would bring him a little closer to the world of the child, a world where at first *everything* is an unknown and is to be made sense of. The most obvious situation for the adult analogous to that of the child is the adult's experience of a context in which the language used is entirely unknown to him. Let us imagine, for example, the average Englishman travelling in Greece or India or China. What is interesting here is to observe *where* the difficulties arise. If, for example, we send our Englishman to buy vegetables in a market he may well do quite an effective job, despite his inability to speak Greek or Hindi or Cantonese. Because he is an adult with experience of his own community, he does have a knowledge of a wide range of *contexts*. All Englishmen have some knowledge of buying and selling, of money and goods, and the ideas of exchange and value. Many Englishmen perhaps could make good use of one part of the interaction going on in the marketplace, for whereas they would not understand the verbal part of the interaction, they might well be able to make sense of the non-verbal part, the gestures, the pointing, the shrugging of shoulders, the shaking of heads, the walking away. Thus, by using his knowledge of buying and selling *in his own community* together with what he knows about the way human beings behave, our Englishman could probably cope quite well with this situation even though he does not have access to the language in question. He would be using for this, however, experience which a child simply does not have. The cumulative experience of buying and selling, of value and exchange, as well as his experience of interpreting the non-verbal behaviour which invariably accompanies face-to-face language activity, all of which is taken for granted by the adult, *is not available to the child*. In a comparable situation, the child has to work to master the whole of this complex inter-relationship of language, concept and action. What for the adult is 'obvious' is, for the child, the product of years of hard work.

Assuming that our adult has been successful in the market place we might interview him to find out a little more about *how* he managed. It is likely that in this context an Englishman would comment on the 'excitability' of the Greeks or the 'inscrutability' of the Chinese. What this information leads us to focus upon is the idea that, though certain elements of non-verbal behaviour were recognised by our Englishman, he did not consider them as being 'the same' as those he was accustomed to in his own community. To him the exuberant way the Greeks use their hands, arms and shoulders when bargaining would seem very much more demonstrative than his own limited use of his hands to convey meaning. Similarly he might well find the limited use of facial expression by the Chinese was so much *less* than his own use of facial movements as to seem to him devoid of any 'expression' at all. There is as wide a variation between communities in the patterns of their non-verbal behaviour as there is between the patterns of the individual languages those communities speak. Moreover, these differences in the patterns of non-verbal behaviour emphasise the fact that what the child does learn is very closely tied to the community in which he must learn it.

At this point, let us return to our Englishman abroad. Having coped fairly successfully with the activities of the market place, let us now imagine him seated at a formal lecture on agricultural methods. Here he is not required to participate, merely to listen. Virtually the entire language activity of the situation is *linguistic*, that is, the language activity provides minimal clues to its meaning beyond the patterns of the language itself, patterns which are wholly unavailable to the listener in this case. Even if there are photographs of yams and mounds, rice plants and paddy fields, tobacco leaves and drying racks, how can he make the connections between these things and the sounds the lecturer utters? One might go a stage further and submit this adult to a lecture on company law, or Marxism, or predestination, subjects where little by way of visual aid could be provided. At this point, our adult would have one thing in common with the human infant, the meaning of the language activity in its entirety would be inaccessible to him. Only from the repetition and demonstration which is a part of everyday life in a normal human environment can the child start to make some kind of sense from a whole series of related unknowns. It is through experiencing the pattern and repetition of events around him, and in being drawn into these events, that a child can begin to make sense of the relationship between these events and the language activity that occurs in conjunction with them. Only in this way can an abstract idea like 'cleanliness' be conveyed to a very young child through newspapers and orange juice. A half hour's explanation, however well meant, would fail with the child, just as a lecture in a foreign language fails for an adult who does not have access to the particular set of meanings which we call a language.

3. 'He didn't say a word'

In the second section of this chapter we said something about the immense task which confronts every child in the course of learning language. By asking the reader to imagine situations where his accumulated knowledge of his own language and his experience of its use was only marginally useful to him, we hoped to show the scale of the task the child undertakes. What is involved goes far beyond a mere facility to reproduce the sounds and patterns of sounds that the child continuously hears about him. These patterns of sounds must be related to patterns of 'meanings' and it is only by a child's involvement in the language activity of concrete situations that he can make for himself the crucial connection between sounds and meanings. Even the patterns of non-verbal behaviour, the varied movements and gestures of face and body that are so essential an element in the total pattern of 'meanings' our language creates, have to be learnt by the child.

If we accept that language learning is indeed a complex activity, and if we also accept and admire the great success of the majority of children in coming to terms with it, then it is not unreasonable for us to ask why it is that children who have performed quite remarkable feats of learning can on occasions discover that they are unable to find language. It is upon this inability to find language to meet particular situations that this last section is focused.

If we are to consider why a system fails to operate we must consider first of all how the system operates in the first place. In this case what we must look at is the way in which human beings process their experience of the world, because their knowledge of how to use language in any particular situation derives from their total experience of the world.

Let us begin by looking again at the world which the human infant encounters at birth. It is a world full of tastes, sounds, shapes, feelings, people and objects. As we said earlier, none of these things are known to the child, he has to 'make meanings' from them and for them. We might almost say that the child has to start making a vast card index system without actually knowing what to write on the cards. There is no doubt that the child does something with all the information he receives from the moment of birth and if to some readers the analogy of a 'card index system' sounds 'inhuman' or 'mechanical', then perhaps we should look briefly at the kind of information given us in recent years by research into the functioning of the brain. In his book, *The Machinery of the Brain*, Dean Wooldridge shows some sympathy towards those who find the idea of the brain as a machine rather an unpleasant one. He says:

'In former times the idea that the heart is no more than a complicated pump, which would one day be replaced by a man-made device during a lengthy surgical operation would have seemed as shocking to most people as the modern discoveries that the brain, too, operates in accordance with the physical laws of nature.'

Wooldridge then goes on to describe how the human brain resembles in some respects the electronic digital computer. He says that what is so important about the computer is that 'complex computational and logical operations can be broken down into steps that can be handled by very simple processing elements'. Another way of putting this is to say that a complex end result can be achieved by a very large number of relatively simple steps.

Most readers of this book will be familiar with the idea that computers can handle vast quantities of information very quickly. What is perhaps not so generally known is that the actual calculations performed by computers are very simple. The impressive end-results produced by the computer are impressive because of the multiplicity of simple actions which the computer can perform very, very quickly. Consider now the enormous volume of information about the world, about people and actions and things, which the child's early years present to him through his membership of a human community. From this continuous flow of experience, at first wholly new and then, frequently, a bewildering mixture of new and old, unfamiliar and familiar, puzzling and certain, he takes what he needs to build up for himself the complex pattern of meanings we imply when we speak of our ability to understand, or to make sense of, the world about us. Only if we assume a truly remarkable capacity upon the part of the brain for recording, sifting, relating and storing the information this experience presents to us can we account for the rapidity with which the child reveals his capacity to interpret his experience accurately.

In itself, this activity upon the part of the child should astonish us, but there is a further point which has to be taken into account when we think of these early years, a point which adds considerable force to the analogy we have drawn between the brain and

22

the computer. Parallel with this process of making 'meanings' out of the information provided by his experience, and intimately bound up with it, the child has been using his capacity to learn language. Indeed, we would suggest that the making of meanings and the learning of language are so closely connected with each other that we ought not to think of two distinct processes, one concerned with meaning and the other with language, but rather one single process in which there is a continuous interplay between meanings and language. The traditional idea that language exists so that we can put our thoughts into words, that language is the dress of, or vehicle for, thought, too readily encourages the parallel idea that language itself is empty of meaning, and that meanings, or thoughts are unmodified by the process of languaging them.

If, then, we accept that the child's learning of his language and his learning to make sense of his experience are but two aspects of one inter-related process, then we can stress the degree to which the growth of this process is absolutely central to the child's activities in his early years. The capacity to interpret the world and to relate to others is dependent upon its successful growth and this capacity is the basis of man's survival as man. As we have suggested, this capacity derives from the way in which the brain possesses a spectacular power to process new information and to store it in significant order for future use. It is for this reason that we suggest that the activity of the young child, in interacting with his experience, results in his creating for himself a marvellously subtle computer-based card index system. What the analogy points to is *how* the child is able to deal with the sheer volume of data experience offers him for processing: needless to say, the analogy does not define *what* he does with the data once he has processed it.

It would be a great help to the argument, if, at this point, the reader would bring to the discussion a very valuable body of research material: the recollection of any occasion on which he or she found it impossible to find the language the situation demanded. It is likely that any reader will be able to recall some such occasion, for the inability to use language in a certain situation is, as we hope to show, a normal feature of the way in which we learn language. The following two examples, taken from my own experience will, I hope, help the reader to make his own list of examples.

On one occasion, some years ago, I was staying with a family in a remote part of Donegal while engaged on some field-work.

Living with the family was an elderly man who had been in poor health for some time. One afternoon as I was getting ready to go out, the daughter of the house, a young woman of about twenty-three, stopped me and asked me to come and look at the old man, whom she thought was not looking well. I followed her into the dark back kitchen, where the old man was sitting by the fire, his pipe in his hand. 'Don't you think he looks paler since yesterday?' she asked. I agreed, but could find nothing else to say, for the old man was dead.

A less terrible situation, but none the less difficult for me, arose when I returned rather late from a whole day outing with a group of fourth-formers. As they gathered their belongings and shouted their 'Goodbye', when the coach stopped outside school, their behaviour was a mixture of high spirits, tiredness and thoughtlessness. Unfortunately, the Headmistress was working late. Next morning, after my own interview with her, I had to deliver a strong reprimand, plus a class detention for their 'unruly behaviour'. At the end of my expostulations a girl appeared at my desk with a large bouquet of flowers and carefully delivered a short vote of thanks for the marvellous outing which they had all enjoyed. The vote of thanks was followed by her request for 'Three cheers'.

Whatever situations the last paragraphs may have recalled for the reader they will all have something in common. Firstly, they will all have involved dealing with other people. Secondly, they will have generated in the reader a feeling that there *was* language available to meet the situation but, at the moment when language was required, it just was not there to hand. One of the most frequent comments made by people who recount experiences such as those I quoted above, is, 'Afterwards, I knew what I should have said'. Another frequent comment is, 'If I had thought of *x* then I would have said *y* but it just didn't occur to me *at the time.*'

This last statement provides a clue to one of the key elements in any situation in which we use language. By using this particular form of words, the speaker implies that there was something in the situation he had overlooked, or had not taken into account, or was quite unaware of *as a factor that could affect his choice of what to say.* It points to the quite crucial fact that, before we can decide *what* to say in a given context we must 'read' the situation. 'Reading' situations is an activity which adults come to do automatically. There are **many** common language phrases which reveal that

24

adults do observe and note many features of the behaviour of others and choose what they say in order to take account of the results of their observations. For example, they 'size-up the situation', they 'take the feeling of the meeting', they 'see how the land lies'. To help them in their observations, adults have both a long experience of reading situations and a long experience of choosing language appropriate to a given situation. What happens when a speaker declares that he was speechless is not that all words 'disappear' in the way that a single word can sometimes do, but that the speaker, or would-be speaker, has either not been able to 'read' the situation, or having 'read' it, is unable to find anything in his experience that would be a guide as to what words would meet the occasion. Using our analogy of the card index system, we could say that a card had been fed into the system reading 'Conversation with Headmaster, what action?' and a print-out returned saying, 'Sorry, no data available.' The result is a situation that very many men and women can still remember with a mixture of dismay and wry amusement many, many years later.

We are always likely to know what to say, therefore, if the cards we feed into the system are cards which have been fed in before. When a situation occurs in adult life, it is often a recurrence, hence we are seldom speechless, because experience is available in the system and will provide us with an appropriate 'tag for action'. It is significant that those men and women who tell the proverbial story of their first encounter with the Headmaster or Headmistress do not in fact tell a 'second meeting' or 'third meeting' story. However difficult these meetings may have been, they certainly lacked the total newness of the famous first occasion. These subsequent encounters had something to draw upon, and even if the tag then available for linguistic action was incomplete or inadequate, there was at least a tag available.

What we are trying to show is that language and experience are both necessarily products of the individual's life as a member of a human community. By participating in innumerable social situations a child learns to use language: it also learns to read situations. It cannot use language in vacuo; and if it cannot read the situation, it cannot use language effectively. The result of this is that sooner or later a human being will meet a situation new enough to find him with no relevant experience 'in store', situations like the two incidents which rendered this writer speechless. What it is important to see is that it is not children only, or boys and girls, or 'the less able', or *any* one group of human beings, who encounter occasions when they cannot find the language they need, it is *all* well-formed human beings, regardless of age, or ability, or experience.

If we can accept this 'failure' as a simple fact of life, rather than as a value judgment, or as a source of anxiety, we will be in a position to make use of the valuable information about our capacity to language that this particular facet of human behaviour gives to us. What it shows us is that we can most easily use language in those contexts with which we are totally familiar; and that we can least easily use language in those contexts with which we are totally unfamiliar. It would also seem that the more often we have to cope with the new and the unfamiliar the more adept we become at coping with it 'on our feet'. Who has not said to himself at one time or another, 'Well, I never saw myself coping with that', or 'I had an awful time at the beginning, but now it doesn't bother me at all.' Most readers of this book will have experienced a period of adaptation to a new situation where new ways of speaking were needed, like going to a secondary school or to an institute of higher education. There may well have been 'speechless' occasions to begin with, but ultimately these were probably overcome, because enough time was available for the reader to build up the necessary experience in the contexts concerned. For the writer, the task of presenting an account of my own class-room work with *Language in Use* to audiences of teachers, showed me clearly that years of teaching and lecturing were only of marginal assistance to me when I was asked *for the first time* to talk about my own work. I might well have been 'speechless' had I not had advance warning of this new task or had I not had a number of friends on whom I could 'practise'.

To sum up, then, we can say that, if a child is born into a community in one part of the world at one moment in time, it will learn the ways of speaking and the ways of behaving of that group of people at that time. It will learn to make sense of the world and to learn language simultaneously. The two processes will be intimately related to each other and the whole experience will be stored by the brain, perhaps like a card index system, but certainly in such a way as to make it possible for the individual to make use of the information he has stored in order to meet the needs of the recurrent human situations in which he finds himself called upon to act and to language. What the child has available in this index is the result of its accumulated experience of its own

26

community. The store can be large or small in comparison to what is potentially available in that community, but what it cannot be is all-inclusive. There will always be situations occurring for that child in that community which are 'unknown' to it, that constitute a 'first time ever' in terms of its already existing experience.

For those of us who are concerned with teaching and learning, 'speechlessness' is a major concern. It is one of the main themes of this book to show that, though we may want to control this 'speechlessness', we can only do this by a fuller understanding of how language works, an understanding which has no place for the idea of 'failure' in relation to the child's, or the pupil's, inability to find language appropriate to the demands of the situations we put him in.

2 Community

1. What do we mean by 'community'?

The trouble about the word 'community' is that we all know what it means, or, more accurately, we can all derive from our individual experience of our own community a meaning for this word. It is not surprising that this should be the case, because 'community' is a common language word like 'school' or 'teacher' or 'kindness' or 'teatime', and the specific 'meaning' any one of us gives to such words as these arises from the particular experience we have had. In a society as complex and diverse as ours, these words can refer to a very wide range of 'meanings'. Before we go on to discuss 'community', therefore, a word about the relationship between words and meanings would be helpful to the argument. To some readers, it may perhaps seem that too great an emphasis is being laid on the fact that words mean what we have learnt them to mean. To them, it is 'obvious' that 'house' means 'house' and 'tree' means 'tree'; and that meaning difficulties only occur when one is dealing with non-standard language, or with a local dialect or with an uneducated or unintelligent person. Many years of field work in different communities, and many years of teaching in different schools, have lead me to a much less optimistic view of our general ability to share meanings with others. For example, when a mother says to a child in a working-class street in Oldham, a nineteenth-century industrial town near Manchester, 'Go in the house', she is in fact sending the child into the main room of the dwelling. 'The house' in this case *means* 'living-room' and it is not surprising that infant teachers in Oldham report that children, when they first come to school 'cannot draw houses'. Some of these teachers are happy when, some weeks later, these same infants are drawing detached houses with four windows, a central door and a tree growing outside, despite the fact that, as
28

one Oldham teacher put it to me, 'They all live in two-windowed terraced houses and there isn't a tree for miles!' What these children have done is to learn a new meaning for 'house', because 'house' at school is different from 'house' at home.

There is a similar tale to tell with 'tree'. Talking to an old man in a desolate part of Western Ireland I said conversationally, 'I suppose it is because of the wind that you have so few trees?' 'Ah, no, miss,' he replied. 'It's the size of the houses. Sure they're so small they have no need of more trees.' He was, in fact, referring to parts of the timber framework of the roof of his house, the only 'trees' with any relevance to his world. Let me offer one final example, one in which it is hoped the reader will participate himself by checking what meaning he himself would give to the chosen words, both now and in his childhood.

Some years ago while I was still teaching in Belfast I was asked to 'cover' an English class for an absent colleague. My instructions were simple; I was to make the group of eleven-year-olds write something. Having asked them what they would like to write about and been told that they didn't like writing because it was too difficult, I decided to try to encourage them by making the writing into a game. We chose three every-day words which they said they could write about and we decided to see at the end of half an hour if they had all written the same thing. The three items chosen were 'tea', 'bun' and 'ticket'. It would not be true to say that we had as many variations as we had eleven-year-olds, but the range of meaning was indeed thought-provoking. 'Tea' to them was everything, from a beverage which some of them did not drink to the name of the main meal of the day, eaten at 6 o'clock in the evening. For some 'tea' was a social occasion which only took place in the context of visiting relatives on Sunday afternoons: for others it was a picnic in the hayfields when they visited country relatives and were given the job of 'taking the men their tea'. My own piece of writing on the life-saving qualities of tea at the end of school was not paralleled by anyone else, even though many of them did in fact have a cup of tea when they arrived home from school. 'Ticket' and 'bun' both produced a similar kind of variation; for some 'ticket' was a necessary feature of getting to school by bus, for others it meant entertainment of every kind from football to ballet, for one it meant her father's parking problems.

It was, however, 'bun' that produced the variation that intrigued the class most. Many of them wrote as I did, about the

29

various kinds of small cakes that are a fairly standard feature of home-baking in Northern Ireland, but one girl baffled the class by saying that she often had a bun with ham in it for supper. She was the only girl in the room who was not born in Northern Ireland and for her 'bun' was a flat bread cake which could be split and filled to make a savoury snack. Had I been engaged in a social survey, the meanings provided by thirty eleven-year-olds would have given me a wealth of information about socio-economic groupings, use of leisure, patterns of eating and social relationships. As it was, it sharpened my awareness of the effect community can have in mediating between a word and its meaning. It is for this reason that throughout this book we will try to be explicit about what we mean, for only by doing this can we give the reader the opportunity to test for himself whether what is being said makes sense.

We begin with a straightforward definition of 'community': a community is a group of people who live in geographical proximity to each other and who, through their work, or worship, or way of life, or any combination of these three, feel a sense of 'us-ness' when they compare themselves with any other group of people. If we break down our definition phrase by phrase we can look more closely at its different elements and see how they fit together. What can we say about geographical proximity? It certainly seems reasonable that if people live near enough to be in daily contact with each other, then they have the opportunity to share a whole range of common experience. There is no doubt that in many areas where community feeling is very well developed, people do in fact live very close to each other in this sense. This is particularly the case in some of the urban, industrial housing areas where a group of tightly packed streets will correspond with a close-knit community life. A recent outstanding account of community life of this kind is to be found in Robert Roberts' account of Salford, Manchester, at the turn of the century, *The Classic Slum* (Penguin). However, if we ask the question, 'Does proximity alone generate community?' the evidence we have would seem to say 'No'. Many British sociologists are concerned with the way people respond to geographical proximity and among these the work of Ruth Durrant is particularly interesting. Ruth Durrant has studied some of the large new housing estates in Britain, where people have been brought together from all parts of the country by the availability of house and jobs. What she says is that, unless there is some common objective, like the

30

improvement of living conditions, or the avoidance of increased rents, then there is no incentive for these people to act together and they do not make contact with each other. On the other hand, where people who already have an active community life are moved to a new estate, as with the London East Enders moved to North London, they will make every effort to maintain their contacts, despite the fact that distances between individuals on the new estates may be much greater than in the previous environment. Much of the unhappiness caused by resettlement has grown from the different meanings of 'nearness', as understood in the community of the people being resettled, and as assumed 'obvious' by the planners.

Why then does proximity not automatically generate community? The answer lies in the other phrases of our definition. Indeed, we would suggest that sharing a geographical location is much less important in terms of human relationships than sharing even the simplest activity or idea. Let us look then at 'work or worship or way of life'.

There is no doubt that some of the most clearly distinguishable communities in Britain grow out of the context of shared work. If we look at the mining villages of Durham or South Wales, at the textile areas of some of the big cities like Manchester or Leeds, at the farming communities, or the small fishing ports, we can see a very strong sense of 'us-ness' at work in them. It is not surprising that a group of people whose life is focused on a mine, a mill, a farm or a boat will share a whole range of activities with those similarly occupied. In particular the traditions of miners are often pointed to as a group expression of the anxieties of a difficult and dangerous activity, where co-operation is an essential part of life. The miner can best share his feelings with another miner, his stories will mean more to another miner, his jokes, his ways of speaking, his view of the world will all make more immediate sense to another miner than to a textile worker, a farmer or a fisherman. It is because of this shared activity that a shared way of thinking about the world, a shared body of assumptions and attitudes towards every aspect of living, develops, and it is the lack of any real basis for shared activity that keeps the housing estate dwellers from making contact with their neighbours.

At this point it is difficult to continue without asking a prior question, 'And how is it that men carry on this shared activity that supports the shared thinking that is the basis of community?'

31

This is an enormous question. For the moment we will offer one part of the answer only in the form of a single remark from the anthropologist, Malinowski:

> '*Language* is the link in concerted human activity.'

In this one sentence, Malinowski requires us to focus unambiguously upon one crucial, and obvious, aspect of community: that man's activities as a social being are possible only because he has language. Moreover, this view of the social function of language is not confined to the more apparent forms of collective activity like mining, fishing or textile working. It also embraces the collective action that expresses our shared feeling with others just as much as our shared work. Perhaps the most immediate example of this is the part religious belief can play in creating the basis of a communities shared experience of the world.

From this point of view, it does not matter whether we consider Jews, Hindus, Catholics, Moslems, Presbyterians, Anglicans, Mormons, or any other of the thousands of named religious groups we have in the world. The common factor in all of them is that those who share a system of belief share also a body of common experience which they do not share with anyone else. We can put it this way: there is a great deal more to religious belief than the joint performance of religious rites, such as we associate with church, mosque, or synagogue. This is because a system of belief, like a religion, is concerned not only with the practice of certain rites but with the events of everyday life. A Jewish woman from a wealthy home, will, if she is a practising Jew, be infinitely easier in the kitchen of a very poor Jewish woman than in the kitchen of a wealthy non-Jewish person. The reason is that in a non-Jewish home she is unlikely to find the two sets of saucepans, without which she cannot observe the Jewish food law which requires that the utensils for preparing milk and meat be kept separate from each other. Similarly, a Free Presbyterian farmer from the Scottish Isles is going to be very upset by the gaiety of Sunday visitors to his island where a particular kind of solemnity is observed on that day. The reader will certainly be able to supply his own examples, but, whatever the belief concerned, it will show that 'belief' involves individuals in sharing a whole range of attitudes and assumptions about everyday life, that is, the life of the community, and that whether the belief involves the purdah of women, the sacredness of all forms of life, or the sinfulness of eating beans, it is providing a fundamental basis for '. . . con-

32

certed human activity' in the same way as the work of the mine, the mill, the farm or the boat.

Finally, we come to 'way of life'. What we must focus on here is the fact that there are communities in existence in Britain where one can find a very wide range of employment and an equally wide range of beliefs or lack of beliefs, and still apply the term 'community', because the 'us-ness' of our definition is felt by the people concerned. What we have here is something which we might not have been able to find a hundred years ago in Britain: people who have worked out how they want to live their life, what sort of house they want, what facilities they want, what kind of surroundings they want, and they have sought out a place which meets all these requirements. They have chosen to live where they live for reasons which, we can say, form part of their belief system, their basis for taking one view of the world rather than another. For this reason the people they live beside share the same beliefs, because they too have come for the same reasons. There are many examples of this kind of community in the more expensive housing developments in the commuter belts to the north and south of London. In most cases, these communities are uniformly what we can call crudely 'middle-class', partly because they attract people from this socio-economic group and partly because newcomers who choose to come, and who have the requisite economic base to do so, quickly adopt the ways of behaving and the values of the existing community. So instead of sharing work, or religious belief, these people share a body of secular views about how one should live, how one's children should be educated, how one should spend leisure, what sort of possessions one should value, and so on; and this provides that feeling of 'us-ness' which is a defining characteristic of community. These people, like those who share work, or who share belief, will have more in common with each other at a fundamental level than with any other group

So far in this section we have shown that community exists where there is sharing of *either* work or worship or way of life. The extent of what is shared differs widely between communities and there are some communities, perhaps the most close-knit of all, that certainly share *all* the possibilities we have mentioned. Consider, for example, the Scottish, Hebridean, Presbyterian fishermen who share not only their work, and their religious views, but also their small and relatively isolated geographical location, their long history as a sea-faring community, their tradition of story-telling and their hard and demanding way of life, as well as many of the individual features of day to day living, even as detailed as the the stitches used by each fisherman's wife when knitting his heavy wool sweaters, or the custom of offering non-alcoholic drinks to low status visitors and alcoholic drinks to high-status visitors.

This last example leads us to an extension of our original definition of community in order to accommodate the fact that what human beings can share with each other is diverse and complex; and that crucial as is 'work, worship and way of life', in creating human communities, there is much more to be said about the detailed patterning of that context. What the sociologist or anthropologist would say is that a community exists when it is possible to point to a group of people and say that they share a common 'culture'. 'Culture' is another word like 'community' which can be used to mean different things. The sense in which we use it here has been very clearly defined by Sir Edward Tyler, the British anthropologist. He suggests that:

'Culture is that complex whole that includes morals, art, laws, knowledge, belief, custom and any other habits acquired by man.'

Given this definition we can see what an enormous scope for variety this will present from community to community.

Consider two communities we might find in Great Britain. One is a peasant-farming, Catholic, conservative, Irish speaking matriarchal, close-knit community with a tradition now of playing hurley, remaining teetotal and agitating for the increase of hill-farm subsidies. The other is a Methodist, Labour-voting, Welsh-speaking, patriarchal, loose-knit community, occupied with a variety of light industries and much given to drinking, lay-preaching and singing in choirs. Both these communities are invention, but all the elements which go to make them up are real elements which do exist in actual existing communities: what the invention does is show the potential for variation.

It is with this variation in mind that I would now ask the reader to think back to the last part of Chapter 1. We had been talking about the fact that however well-developed a person's capacity to use language might be in one particular context, he might still encounter 'speechlessness' when presented with a 'first time ever' experience in which he was required to use language. What I actually said in Chapter 1 was:

'What a child has available in this index is the result of its accumulated experience of its own community. The store can be large or small in comparison to what is potentially available in that community, but what it cannot be is all-inclusive. There will always be situations occurring for the child in that community which are "unknown" to it, that constitute a "first time ever" in terms of existing experience.'

What I would now want to add to that statement in Chapter 1 is a further comment, a comment which the theme of this first part of Chapter 2 has tried to clarify. It is:

and what will meet the child's needs for living and working in *one* community may have little relevance to meeting the needs of living and working in another.

Much more will be said about this particular question. What we must now go on to consider in the next section is how it is that a group of people, living in a particular place, at a particular time, create by their constant interaction with each other, and with the world outside, a way of seeing, a way of thinking, and a way of languaging that is so intimate and personal to that community that an outsider can meet the linguistic demands of the situations he encounters in that community only with difficulty and practice, even though he possesses the same mother tongue, and indeed inhabits the same city or town or village.

2. Learning to be a member of your own community.

'No, John, don't hit Helen, she's your sister. No, John, don't hit Stephen he's smaller than you. John, let Stephen play with your truck, you mustn't be selfish. No. Don't load it up with mud. You'll get all dirty. Helen, put that gun away. Little girls don't play with guns. Where is your doll's pram?'

Most readers will be able to place fairly easily the context in which the foregoing piece of monologue was recorded. A 'middle-class' mother in a suburban garden is intervening in the play of three children under five. What this mother is *doing* is something which is done by every adult who regulates the behaviour of a child, whether that adult is an East European 'babuska', a Samoan mother, an aborigine father, or a children's nurse from any country the reader may choose to name. What the mother is *saying* is a very different matter and we shall consider that a little later on.

At this point in our discussion, it is quite impossible to separate 'language' from our thinking about 'community', even temporarily, because it is through the use of language by adults that a child both learns his language and 'learns his community'. The adults in a child's environment provide him with a constant supply of information as they go about their everyday affairs. They already exist in a group with established relationships and ways of speaking and they draw the child into this world by interacting with him. The word 'interact' is not here used as another way of saying 'talk to'. If children were only 'talked to', they would remain very much in the position of the adult in the last chapter who attended the lecture on agricultural methods delivered in a foreign language. 'Interact' means a great deal more than this for it insists that we treat *all* language activity between people, face-to-face, as activity which involves a two-way process. Here, it implies that we must see the child involved in a dialogue in the course of normal everyday events where he is encouraged to respond, and where his response is listened to or observed. The encouragement to respond may indeed come in the form of the kisses and cuddles of the baby-books, but it is just as likely to involve impatience, or irritation, or sharp command. What is important for the child is that these responses should be made available to him so that he can experience them in the context of his own actions. It would be fair to say that the really deprived child is not the one who has to tolerate a high degree of fairly harsh regulation, but the child who is ignored, left alone, tidied away, for this child is the one deprived of that constant stream of feed-back upon his own words and actions which adults alone can supply in the course of their interaction with him.

The extract with which I began this section is an example of using language to regulate behaviour. It relates to one mother in one particular community, but it is at the same time representative of that 'constant stream of feed-back' that adults supply to children in *all* communities. It is from the information this feed-back supplies that the child not only learns his language in terms of its semantics, grammar and phonology, but learns also the values of the community in which he lives, because these values are embedded in the language.

How can this be so? How can a language carry the values of a community in such a way that learning a language automatically involves learning a set of values? Let us look now at what the middle-class mother was *saying* as she regulated the play of the three children and take each sequence in turn.

'No John don't hit Helen, she's your sister. No John, don't hit Stephen, he's smaller than you.'

36

This mother is expressing the view that there should not be discord between brothers and sisters; and that hitting someone smaller than yourself is unacceptable behaviour. We have to say that here, in however simple a form, she is expressing a moral view about the use of physical violence against others and the possible recipients of such violence. John will have to find out on another occasion whether he can, in fact, hit someone who is (*a*) the same size as he is; (*b*) bigger than he is; (*c*) a girl, but not his sister.

'No don't load it up with mud, you'll get all dirty.'

Here the mother is expressing a view regarding what is appropriate and what is not. One might draw from her words the simple conclusion that dirty clothes mean more work for mothers. However, in an age of washing machines and anthropological studies of the symbolic meaning of everyday things this seems too simple a view. As far as we know, no human community is without its taboos on dirt, although what constitutes 'dirt' varies from community to community. One might hazard a guess that this particular mother associates dirty hands and faces with a social group with which she does not want to be associated through the actions of her children. All that we wish to do here is to show that a commonplace command about getting dirty may carry much more symbolic significance for the speaker, and hence have a much deeper meaning for the child, than the mere surface sense of the words spoken might suggest.

'Helen put that gun away. Little girls don't play with guns. Where is your doll's pram?'

In this final comment the mother expresses another view of 'rightness'. In her world, boys play with guns, girls play with doll's prams, just as in a very different community girls concern themselves with digging sticks and boys with bows and arrows. 'Gun' for this mother must have a powerful meaning to provoke such an immediate response. It might be fair to suggest that gun/doll's pram represents concretely for this mother a much deeper categorisation of feelings and emotions than simply what John and Stephen and Helen can play with. In her value system little girls should be 'tender', 'sensitive', 'soft' or 'made of sugar and spice and all things nice' perhaps, as the nursery rhyme and the main stream of woman's magazines would have it. They should not demonstrate aggressiveness, forcefulness, or strong control over others for these are the attributes of little boys. In this context, the gun is a symbol for the mother of all those ways of behaving that her culture leads her to assess as proper for males. So she reacts to 'gun' and substitutes 'doll's pram', for 'doll's pram' in its turn is an objective correlative for those values which this mother wishes her daughter to acquire in forming her view of herself as a female in this same culture.

In this action our South Manchester, suburban, middle-class mother is behaving as any other mother in the same social group might behave. She might well be surprised to find that her action would be fully understood and sympathised with by adults in vastly different communities. For example, there are many hunting tribes where a girl-child touching any object connected with hunting requires an elaborate ritual for avoiding the bad luck that is believed to follow from such an action. This is not the place to explore further why it is that all human groups make the kind of categorisations represented by the gun and the doll's pram in this instance. The universality of this connection between rules and meanings, however, is what we need to recognise, because such rules and their meanings are perpetuated by being passed on through the language used to control each succeeding generation. In this way each adult participates actively in perpetuating the values of the community to which he belongs.

If we take another extract, one which is far removed, geographically and socially, from the one we have been using we can illustrate this similarity of adult action, a similarity that can well be concealed by the vast dissimilarity in what the two adults are actually saying. The following extract was recorded in an area of run-down nineteenth-century housing near the Belfast school where I used to teach.

'What's wrong with you then, whinging there in the house, away out and play—who hit you—Willie Taggart indeed—well why didn't you hit him a kick, yer as big as he is—stand up for yerself and be a man—d'ye want everyone to think yer a wee girl?'

From what this mother says to her child we can in fact work out that she responds to violence quite differently from the mother in our earlier example. For this mother, the use of violence towards others is a defining characteristic of 'being a man'. In fact, we can go so far as to say that she makes it obligatory for her son to demonstrate his manliness by 'hitting Willie Taggart a kick'. Failure to do this will make him into a 'a wee girl', an object of
38

derision in his family, in the street, and in the community at large. By implication, it also tells us something about the relative status of men and women in that community, judged merely as male and female. The pressure on the child to accept this norm for his behaviour is overwhelming and it is difficult for the writer, so familiar with the widespread occurrence of this attitude to violence not to point to the Belfast of the early 1970s as an example of the terrifying effectiveness of patterns of language in shaping subsequent patterns of action.

However, whatever one may feel about the values being presented by the two mothers I have quoted, what is important to the argument is to see that the two mothers are indeed *doing* the same thing. They are teaching their children to behave in a way that will identify them as members of the group into which they have been born and they are doing this by using words and phrases that express concretely the values their community has attached to them. Intuitively, both mothers will try to eliminate behaviour that does not 'fit' the values of their community, for the more fully the child learns and accepts the values of the community the more easily will he be accepted as fully a member of it.

All human communities, therefore, find it necessary to use language in this way in order to bring children into the group. In some communities, it is the mother who performs the largest part of the task and it so happens that the examples used above do both focus upon the mother. This situation, however, is not universal. Patterns of child care vary from community to community and in some cases the mother is of little significance; grandmother, aunt or nurse being the key figure. Whatever the actual local situation might be, however, it is important to see that *all* the adults with whom the child has contact contribute to his understanding of the world by demonstrating their attitudes to the events of everyday life. In some groups, the process of bringing children into the community is carried out intuitively by adults. They treat the children in the way that they were themselves treated as children, because this is the 'obvious' or 'natural' or 'only' way to treat them. This is not the case, however, with many of the social groups which exist in the advanced industrial countries like Britain or the U.S.A. In these countries, many adults are well aware of what membership of a particular social group involves and they may go to extreme lengths to ensure that their children identify themselves with the community concerned. This has been a marked feature of many of the immigrant groups

39

from Europe who have established a new home in the U.S.A. It is also demonstrated by the great expense incurred by English middle and upper class parents to ensure that their children's education will give them the 'right' accent, and the 'proper' way of speaking so that there is no danger of them being identified with any group other than their own.

This whole process of bringing the newcomer into the community, this need to ensure that he is taught the rules and meanings by which a community expresses its collective identity, is the process to which contemporary sociology has given the name 'socialisation'. As we have seen, from the point of view of the relationship between language and community, it is a quite crucial process. 'Socialisation' means, literally, 'the making social of', where 'social' means, not 'friendly' or 'sociable', as in the common language, but rather 'able to act in the society of other human beings', or 'able to function in a social context'. Socialisation, from the point of view of John, Stephen and Helen and the nameless victim of Willie Taggart means that they know what is acceptable and unacceptable in the course of their everyday life. They know that 'selfish' is not sharing with others; they know that you do not load mud into a dumper truck when wearing the shoes called 'best'; they know what they should do when faced with the question of using physical force towards others. The process of socialisation has provided them with the capacity to act in the everyday situations which form part of their world. It will be clear to the reader that the more fully informed the child is about the ways of behaving in his community, or, put another way, the more successfully he has been socialised, the easier life will be both for the child and for the community of which he is a member. On the other hand, the more closely a child is socialised into one community the more likely he is to encounter difficulty in adjusting to living in any community other than his own.

It might seem to some readers that the last two sentences constitute part of an argument 'for' or 'against' socialisation. This is not the case As far as this book is concerned socialisation is a fact of life, a fact similar in kind to the failure to meet linguistic needs we spoke of in the last chapter. Socialisation describes an inescapable part of the process of learning to be human, because it describes the consequences of the necessary interaction between the growing child and his only source of explicit information about the world, the adults who surround him and make his survival possible. It is for this reason, therefore, that we must try

40

to understand how socialisation works and what its effects are. If we have any doubts about the importance of the part it plays in the development of the young human being then we have only to consider the sad plight of the autistic child to see what happens if a child is unable to enter into the socialising process.

3. Seeing as the community sees

In the first section of this chapter we focused upon the idea of 'community' and looked at the way in which communities can be so very different from each other while at the same time functioning in such very similar ways. A key concept in this section was the idea that members of a community share a common culture. In the second section we focused upon the way in which newcomers are socialised, thereby ensuring the continuity of the community and its culture.

This final section shows, therefore, how it is that the process of socialisation not only gives the child access to the set of meanings which we call language but also provides him with a set of values, what we might describe as the 'meanings' which realise the culture of the community in terms of possible ways of behaving. Let us begin by focusing again on the process of socialisation.

What makes the task of understanding the process and effect of socialisation so difficult is that we all, both writers and readers, have been socialised, and so understanding this process involves our focusing upon something which is not 'out there', but something which both intimately affects each one of us and of which we may be relatively unaware. For the present writer, one small incident, recurring regularly, helps to remind me of the power of early socialisation. As a child, brought up in the shadow of a strict Scottish Presbyterian, Sunday observance, I was forbidden to manicure my nails on a Sunday. Now, many years later, I still find myself pausing to remember the day when I pick up a nail file or emery board. When such a trivial incident as this can still convey a whole set of meanings after twenty years, what other deeply held notions persist without my full awareness? Perhaps the reader will test this for himself by considering for a few moments some small consequences of his own socialisation. The following questions may be a useful prompt in helping the reader to assess his own experience from this point of view. Those questions that seem quite irrelevant will at least serve the purpose of indicating what was *not* important or significant in his community.

Who did you play with as a child? With all children or with some? If you played with some, why not others? Were they too dirty/too snobbish/too far away/not like us/too old/too badly-spoken? Did you play equally with boys and girls? If not, why was this so?
Were you allowed to play every day?
Who were you permitted to hit?
Were you permitted to lend or borrow possessions?
Were you permitted to cry, to talk when you felt like talking, to get dirty, to kiss, to refrain from kissing?

The answers to these, and to many thousands of such questions, will be available to the reader, or certainly were available to him in childhood, for without a long, long, list of answers a child would not be able to cope with even the most seemingly 'simple' and 'obvious' events of everyday life.

Consider, for example the problem of this three year old. While shopping with her mother in a large supermarket, she is offered a peeled banana by a smiling man in a white coat. Mother is preoccupied with soap-powders and the little girl is quite baffled. The fact that she likes bananas does not help her to assess this situation. Her knowledge of 'taking things' is not adequate for this occasion. Fortunately, at the critical moment, the information supply returns: 'Say, "Thank you" to Mr Jones, Lisa', is accompanied by friendly smiles all round which tell Lisa that this person is acceptable and that bananas may be accepted from him. On the next encounter she will not have to recourse to toe-scuffing shyness in order to cover her dilemma. Like all children, Lisa is dependent for her answers on the language used by adults in her presence: it is from this language, item by item, piece by piece, that she must extract the information she needs, both to master the language for herself and at the same time to master the complexities of social action in her own community. What Lisa must do is build up her knowledge of the culture. Yet we have defined culture as a complex whole that includes morals, art, law, knowledge, belief, and custom—and it may seem to the reader an impossibly long way from a three-year-old's dilemma over a banana in a supermarket to a definition of culture such as this. I must try, however, to show that complex cultural attitudes are involved even in such a 'simple' everyday situation. For example, in the particular community we have been speaking of, the giving of gifts is part of a reciprocal system. A gift may be given in return for a favour of some kind where money would be considered an inappropriate way of acknowledging the debt. A mother may give flowers or chocolates to someone who has looked after the children but who is not a recognised 'baby-sitter': a man might give a bottle of whisky to a friend who had 'spoken' for him in finding a job or a house. But for anything given, there is the implicit idea of an appropriate return. Now, a person giving a banana to a child he knows has his return in the response of the child and of its mother. The gift reinforces the mutual exchange of friendly gestures between the adults concerned. But what of the stranger? His gift to the child would cause anxiety in this community, because, as he does not know the mother, there cannot be the same exchange of friendly gestures. The view of reciprocity held by the community and acquired concretely by the child will raise the question 'What does he want from me in return?' Perhaps we can put it more sharply by asking the reader to work out, from the information given above, what the response would be in this community if a male stranger were to give a gift to this child's attractive mother? So we see that the apparently simple act of giving a banana to a child is in fact an action governed by the morals, beliefs and customs of the community.

Let us try to sum up the significance of this example. We are saying that a child must learn his culture if he is to function successfully in the social situations that make up his active experience of his community. Elsewhere, Tyler suggests that we can think of all the rules and meanings by which a culture is made concrete for the members of a particular community as 'the habits of the tribe'. We can extend this remark and think of an advanced industrial society like our own as a 'tribe of tribes', so that a child has the initial task of learning the habits of his own tribe, or community. At some stage, however, often very early, he is made aware of the fact that 'they' exist: 'they' being the verbal embodiment in his local and particular world of the 'morals, art, law, knowledge etc.' of the larger world of the society of which his own community is but one 'tribe'. At this point, we must recognise the limitations of space and the scope of this book. We cannot go on to show how all the elements in Tyler's definition might be realised concretely in the child's immediate experience and how this would show up in the language activity associated with his learning his culture. Instead we must use the remaining space in this chapter to consider how the sharing of a common culture can affect the members of a community in their contact with the outside world. Let us consider the following.

'Course 'e beats 'is wife, she's 'is wife ain't she? S'only natchral.'

'But my dear, positively no-one goes into town without a hat. It just isn't done.'

'No, now you can't do that at all. Shure isn't that the west side? Whoever heard of anyone building on the west side?'

Here we have three utterances expressing the views of three different speakers on the subject of wife-beating, hat-wearing and house-extending. What the three speakers have in common is a supreme confidence in the truth of what they are saying. The first speaker does not doubt that beating one's wife is appropriate behaviour any more than the second speaker doubts that wearing a hat is appropriate behaviour. The third speaker is similarly convinced that extending a house on the west side is quite unthinkable. It is highly likely that readers of this book may doubt the 'truth' of one or all of these statements, because their own 'truth' is different from what these three have said. What concerns us here, however, is why the speakers express the view that they do and why they are so confident that their view is the only possible one. The answer lies in their communities. All three speakers come from close-knit communities where the view recorded here is shared by everyone. In this case, 'everyone' must be noted as 'everyone in the community', just as 'no-one' must refer to people who are not members of the community. It is palpably untrue that 'no-one' is ever seen in a British town or city without a hat, but it is equally true that there was a time when 'no-one' of a particular social group would indeed allow herself to be seen hatless in the West End of London. If everyone in a community holds the same view, then this view becomes for them the relevant 'truth', because they 'can't conceive' of any alternative mode of action.

In the writer's own culture there is a saying that 'what you never have you never miss'. Basically, the sense of this saying is that, if you have not experienced something you do not miss it, or feel the lack of it. It would seem that the absence of any alternative view of a subject is not missed, indeed not even suspected, by members of a community, and so their view of the case takes on the lineaments of an unquestionable rightness. For example, when the third speaker, a peasant farmer in Western Ireland, wanted to build an extra bedroom on his two-roomed house, he did not even consider building on the west side. Having assured me that 'nobody ever builds on the west side', it took a lot of tactful

44

questioning to reveal that in this community there is a belief that fairy paths always avoided houses by passing on the west side; and that to build across a fairy path would bring bad luck on the whole dwelling. Despite the fact that this farmer also said he did not believe in fairies, he still refused to build on the west side, because it 'just wouldn't be right'.

All adults necessarily hold at least some deeply held views similar to the three views we have quoted above, but children as young as two or three years old already hold well-formed views of the same kind. Indeed, if they did not, they would be quite at a loss in relating themselves to the intimate world of the family around them. Because they cannot yet handle their language well enough to express these views in a way that an adult can easily recognise is not to be taken as a sign that they do not possess the cultural information which is the basis of social decision making. For those of us concerned with teaching and learning, it is not enough to guess at what view a child may be taking of the situations which it encounters in our presence. If we cannot find out from the child himself how he views what we are trying to do, what he considers 'right' or 'natural' or 'obvious', then we must go beyond the class-room and seek the information we need in the child's community. From his community, the child derives the culture upon which he bases his view of the world. If we remain ignorant of that view, our alternative view, especially perhaps our alternative view of school and learning, will defeat all our best endeavours to understand, or to teach, a child who comes from any community other than the one we know most intimately—our own.

3 Language, the individual and his view of the world

1. How we 'see' our world

It is a commonplace of our everyday experience that 'No two people think alike' and an equally common experience that no two people view an event in exactly the same way. Yet here we are maintaining successfully a vast range of 'concerted human activity', living and working in the context of communities that can exist only in so far as we are able to think like each other and to view events from a common standpoint. What we want to explore in this chapter is the apparent contradiction revealed by these two familiar experiences. If we take the first of these experiences and press it too far, we find we have to insist that language is a very poor means of conveying meanings from one person to another. This is a position adopted by a number of contemporary writers, in particular, Samuel Beckett. We are then left with the problem of accounting for, or arguing away, the apparent success with which human beings *do* manage to reach common agreement, time after time, about a multitude of everyday events. On the other hand, if we insist upon language as a means of communication, and take a rather simple view of the meanings involved in that activity, we may well seem to present a picture of language activity so simple that there is no room for our common experience of misunderstanding, or misinterpreting, the words of others. If we are to understand the part language plays in community, and community in maintaining language, then we must offer an account of language as both the means, and the product, of concerted human activity, an account which avoids both the nihilism of the contemporary writer and the glib optimism of the communications engineer.

Let us begin by taking the commonest of examples, one that every reader will be able to match only too well from his own experience. Let us say there has been a fight in the playground and two boys arrive to give their views as to what has happened:

'He came up and shoved me, sir!'
'No I didn't. I just somehow bumped into him and he hit me.'
'I didn't hit him, sir. I just shoved back.'

And so on. Let us say that no question of dishonesty or deceit is involved. Neither of the lads are trouble-makers and they genuinely want to tell the truth *as they see it*. The first and obvious point is that they use different key terms, 'bump' and 'shove'. Both of them accept implicitly that violent physical contact has to be accounted for, but, while they both accept that 'shove' is an aggressive act, justifying retaliation, it looks as if this is the only interpretation the boy who speaks first has available for violent contact of this kind. To him, it must be intentional, therefore aggressive. To the other boy, however, there is an alternative possibility: that collision in a crowded playground can be accidental, and therefore is not culpable. We could say that his ability to choose between 'bump' and 'shove' in accounting for his actions opens up to him an alternative way of seeing the events not available to the other. Had we more text to consider, we might be able to show that this incident implied a deep difference in the way in which the two boys see the world, a difference ultimately related to their different experience of community. We could suggest that the first boy's experience of violent physical contact was such that he 'could not conceive' of its being other than intentional, while the second boy's experience might well suggest that contact of this kind was to be construed as unintentional until proved otherwise.

When we consider the varying reports one reads of a road accident, a political speech, a new film or play, it certainly seems that there is more to 'seeing' than a matter of eyesight or lighting conditions. Even if it were a question of vision in the literal sense we must remember how much of our ability to interpret visual perceptions is a matter of learning *what* to see. It is not the eye that 'sees' but the brain, and the brain has to learn how to see. People, blind from birth, who have had their eyesight restored by surgery cannot in fact 'see'. They have to be taught to make sense of the unrelated shapes and colours which for them do not have meaning. In some sad cases, they have finally been unable to do this. For those of us who do have sight, what we 'see' does have meaning, but that meaning has been learnt in the course of our growing up. Meaning is something which we create by using language to interpret our experience of the world. How we 'see' the things around us, therefore, is very much a product of our using the language that others already use in the environment in which we find ourselves. When we 'see' things, the 'seeing' is a product of our own experience, hence one boy's long experience of shoving and being shoved leads him to see a particular event as a shove, while the other boy, with a different body of experience to draw upon sees it as a bump.

We can also say that our 'reading' of a situation will be affected by our experience, just as our seeing is so affected. 'Reading' a situation is something we all do, but we are not always conscious of doing it much as we are not always conscious of what it is we are doing when we report that we 'see'. Only if subsequently we have to recount an incident are we really aware of what we have been doing, as with the following account recently overheard on a London bus.

'Oh yes, poor old dear, all alone she was, must have gone off in her sleep. Oh such a time as we had with her son and the police and all. You see I saw her milk-bottle on Monday, and I says to myself, I says, "Old Mrs Smith's having a bit of a lie in this morning, she is." Well the milk was still there in the evening and I says to Elsie, "I reckon Mrs Smith's gone off to 'er sister for the day", for she sometimes does, you know, sudden like, for 'er sister's been poorly. Well, then Tuesday comes and I'm going out on the early shift and there it still is, and I thinks to myself, "Ron, there's something wrong here", and I goes back and tells Elsie to phone 'er son for we didn't have a key—and sure enough when I gets back its all over—poor old dear.'

Ron has read the situation represented to him by the presence of an uncollected bottle of milk outside the flat of an elderly lady. Because of his previous experience, the milk bottle has meaning. He reads the meaning on Monday morning as 'Mrs Smith's having a bit of a lie in'; on Monday evening, he reads the changed meaning as 'Mrs Smith's gone to her sister's for the day'; and then on Tuesday, he reads a new and serious meaning in the continued presence of the milk-bottle outside the flat and makes the prediction that all is not well. His reading of the situation, based on his previous experience of the old lady's habits, enables him to make a prediction which proves to be quite correct. We can say then that both what we 'see' and what we 'read' are based on our use of our previous experience in a particular way; and

48

that our expectations will help us to shape what we do see and read. For example, a bank manager presented with the barrel of a gun, a masked man and a demand for money, will expect an attempt at robbery; he is unlikely to expect either a student rag-day joke or a police-sponsored test of his security arrangements. Similarly a teacher, presented with a 'stupid' child, will expect its silence to indicate an incapacity to answer rather than a capacity to think.

George Kelly, the American psychologist we spoke of in Chapter 1, has a great deal to say about these 'expectations' which we form. He puts forward the idea that man is 'a problem-solving animal'; that day-to-day living involves us in a process of continuous problem solving at every level, from the most trivial to the most serious. As the reader reads this book he may solve the problem of bodily stiffness by changing position or stretching his legs: he may solve the problem of mental tiredness by pausing to look out of the window, or going to make a cup of coffee. These actions are not thought about in any detail, because they have been used before by the reader to solve similar problems. If a cup of coffee, or a break, has in the past refreshed a particular reader, then he predicts that this action will fulfill his needs again should he encounter a similar situation. Kelly suggests that man is in business to make sense of the world around him; and that his major task is to test the sense he has formulated against the events he encounters. It is as if man is continually 'reaching out and beating the world to the punch': his need is to be able to anticipate what is going to happen next so that he can have a plan for action, already prepared, according to his predictions of the likely outcome.

This idea would certainly seem to fit some of the illustrations we have already used in this book. Victoria in Chapter 1, page 18, at the age of eighteen months, predicts that the spreading of news-paper will facilitate the production of orange drink. Earlier in this chapter, the man on the bus, Ron, makes a series of predictions which he tests against real events. Because he has made relevant predictions, he has also formulated a plan of action which leads to his decision on Tuesday morning to contact the old lady's son.

So one major feature of our ability to read situations in which we find ourselves is our ability to make predictions about the behaviour of others, based upon our previous experience of like situations. This leads us to consider a further aspect of this ability to beat the world to the punch. Kelly suggests that one thing which is 'basic to our making sense of our world and of our lives is our continual detection of repeating themes'. This raises the question as to how we do, in fact, detect repeating themes. What we suggest is that the key to our recognising repeating themes in the world is our use of language, both the way we observe its use by others and the way we use it ourselves, when we 'work things out' inside our heads. For example, the children playing in Chapter 2 are very likely to have experienced repeating themes in the instruction of the adult who was intervening in their play. The individual 'do's' and 'don'ts' themselves were very varied, and the criteria used to judge each action particular to it, but this variation obscures the presence of at least two consistent repeating themes which the children would have picked up from the stream of comment regulating their actions: that relationships with others involve a basic distinction between actions that one is allowed to do and actions that one is forbidden to do; and that what actions are, and are not, do-able in particular circumstances is determined by rules which you cannot work out for yourself from the actions themselves. From the first of these two repeating themes, a child comes to predict that all actions must fall into one of two categories 'do-able' and 'not do-able'. In Kelly's terms, the child will develop a 'construct' based on its observance of this repeating theme in its experience. We have to think of a 'construct' as a working hypothesis which is tested against new experience, but, as in science, testing a hypothesis leads us to look for positive evidence that will verify our predictions. Hence the tester is predisposed to look for things which will confirm his view. This is not to say that he will always overlook negative evidence but the presence of a pre-existing 'construct' is likely to predispose him to 'see', or 'read', new events in terms that will verify or confirm, rather than falsify, his predictions. In this way, we can account for the commonplace that we can so easily 'mistake' the new and interpret it as something familiar to us already. We might add that the ability to accept willingly evidence that falsifies our predictions, that is, asks us to change our minds, is a relatively sophisticated ability. No doubt most readers will be familiar with some version of the story about the eminent member of parliament who said, in reply to a statement of evidence counter to his own opinion, 'Don't confuse me with facts, I've made up my mind'.

Consider for instance what would happen if you, the reader, were to wake up tomorrow morning in total darkness. Assuming that you do not live north of the Arctic Circle and are reading this book in winter, and that you do believe that the sun will rise tomorrow, what would your reactions be? Might you first consider the possibility of your watch or clock misleading you so that it really is still night? Might you consider a solar eclipse, or would you assume *at first waking* that the sun had not risen at its predicted time? In relation to experience of this kind, Kelly considers that we must see ourselves as individuals who

'anticipate events by construing their replication',

so that the reader, waking in total darkness, will draw on his past experiences of waking in darkness and make use of these experiences as the basis for his prediction rather than rely upon the new experience of the sun failing to rise.

If we now take what Kelly has said and relate it to the child learning to be a member of his community we can see that the values, attitudes and assumptions of the community constitute 'repeated themes' for the child. Once he has detected these repeated themes, the child can then use them to develop his own system of constructs, his own way of making satisfactory predictions about the events of his world. It is the child, therefore, who 'reads' the meaning of the themes as they repeat themselves in the language and the actions of others: and it is the child who has to build his own system of constructs, based upon his 'reading' of his experience. It is the community, however, which provides the language and the actions of others, the substance of this experience he abstracts from in his building. To refer back for a moment to our opening paragraph, we can now suggest that 'No two people think alike', because each has built his own system of constructs with which to read the people and events of his experience: but that we have no difficulty in creating and maintaining all our concerted human activity, because the substance out of which we build is shared in common with everyone else who shares a community with us.

The community, through making language available to the child, makes shapes and objects, people and relationships, into 'knowable' things, things which have meaning and can be talked about. Consider any occasion when a group of children or adults have to make sense of some unfamiliar object, be it a geranium or a generator. Notice their relief when someone offers them a name for the object. They do not so much want an account of the workings of the generator, or the structure of the geranium, as a name

51

for a set of recognisable characteristics which can be stored. Once the name is given, 'generatorlikeness' or 'geraniumlikeness' can be added to their repertoire for use on some other occasion when these qualities turn up again in their experience. If a community were to see a similarity between generators and geraniums, because both of these objects were red, then this common feature would come to the children of that community through the way in which the adults joined them together in the language they used for talking about their similarity, rather than their difference.

What, then, would happen if a child who lived in this community which emphasised the similarity between generators and geraniums were to move to another community where generators belonged to the category 'machinery' and geranium to the category of 'plant'? The child's construct would lead him to make predictions about generators and geraniums which would be falsified, because his construct is 'non-transferable'. In Kelly's terms 'a construct has a limited range of convenience', and beyond a certain context it will not hold, that is, any predictions based upon it will be systematically falsified when tested against real events in contexts outside its range of convenience. The first boy in our example at the beginning of this section successfully illustrates this point. He can only construe violent contact as aggressive: in a social context where violence to the person is unthinkable, and such contact can only be accidental, he would find himself operating beyond the 'range of convenience' of his construct. His predictions about the meaning of such contact would be continually falsified by the 'polite' response of others whenever it occurred.

Applying a construct beyond its range of convenience is a major preoccupation of Johnson Abercrombie in her book *An Anatomy of Judgement*. She illustrates the difficulties which arise by quoting the case of a group of medical students who were learning how to read X-ray plates. When the students were told that the X-ray plates were those of tuberculosis patients, the students 'saw' shadows on the plates consistent with this diagnosis, even though the plates were, in fact, entirely clear of such shadows. On the other hand, when they were not given such information about the medical condition of the patients whose plates they viewed, they failed to 'see' shadows which an experienced eye could read very clearly. From her own long experience of situations of this kind Abercrombie develops the idea of 'pre-existing schemata', what the individual brings to the situation in terms of an already worked out scheme or plan of interpretation for the events it contains. Abercrombie's 'schemata', and Kelly's 'constructs' are two ways of approaching the same thing. What they contribute to our present discussion is the idea that human beings do not come to a situation 'fresh', or 'open-minded', or devoid of 'preconceptions', but rather with a well-ordered body of experience from which they derive predictions about anything that relates to it.

That the ordering of this body of experience has to be done through language, and that the language available to the child for this activity will be the language of a particular community, demonstrates the degree to which 'our' view of the world is only 'ours' in a very special sense.

2. Seeing what we expect to see

In the last section, we explored the way in which we build up for ourselves a body of ordered information about the world, derived from our cumulative experience of people, actions and things, a body of information that we then use in order to make predictions about the likely meaning of what happens to us. Clearly, the fact that we do make predictions of this kind certainly does not mean that our predictions are always confirmed by the truth of the events to which we apply them. If all the predictions we made were as 'correct' as their basis in our experience was 'well-ordered', then we would not have in our language a range of expressions like 'dropping a clanger', 'making a boob', 'making a faux-pas', or 'putting one's foot in it'.

Consider the following situation. In the 1930's, a European agriculturalist was employed by a Central African missionary group with a particular concern for the improvement of village agriculture. The expert visited a series of yam-growing villages and noted with horror that the yams were planted in great mounds of earth which had become covered with weeds, because the technique of hoeing was not known. The yield of yams per acre was limited, because mounds were used rather than ridges and furrows. The presence of weeds indicated to the expert, not only a lack of care on the part of the villagers, but also a potential diminution in the fertility of the soil on which the yams were dependent.

With the aid of a team of helpers, the expert organised the weeding and demolition of the inefficient mounds. New crops were planted in parallel rows and hoeing was introduced to keep away weeds. Some weeks later, the first rainstorm of the season produced three inches of rain in as many hours. The furrows between the ridges became small gulleys which eroded the ridges, exposing the newly planted yams, while at the same time carrying off all the carefully loosened top soil to the nearest river.

At one level, the expert is not to be blamed for reading the luxuriant plant growth of the old yam mounds as 'weeds', for it is true that they were not classifiable as food producing plants. What these plants did so very successfully, however, was to reduce erosion by holding the soil together with their roots and by breaking the force of the large raindrops with their foliage. Similarly, the 'inefficient' mound, which reduced the density of plants per acre, was not 'read' by the expert as a conservation device which allowed the villagers to collect what soil was displaced from the top of the mounds from the vegetation traps on their bases and sides and simply return it to the top, a process which was quite impossible when they were faced with hundreds of furrows and ridges and the soil already on its way down river!

We can probably agree that agricultural experts working in Africa ought to make a full study of climatic conditions before 'improving' agriculture, but what concerns us here is to try to see how and why this expert 'got it wrong'. If we consider his 'failure' in terms of what we have said about the work of both Kelly and Abercrombie, we can compare it with the situation we outlined in Chapter 1, when we were considering why, in certain situations, a speaker cannot find the language he needs to meet the demands of a particular situation. We suggested that in many cases this happens to us because we have not had the necessary prior experience of other situations similar to the one in question. Our failure to find the language we need in a situation of this kind is not a sign that we lack some basic capacity to cope with the activity of languaging, therefore, but an indication that, however competent the speaker, there are likely to be new situations occurring for him that will find him 'speechless'. Broadly, we need to accept that well-formed human beings can make sense of what they *have* experienced, certainly in terms of the activities of day-to-day living, so that a failure to do so ought *first* to be considered in terms of the possible newness or unfamiliarity of the experience rather than the weakness or inadequacy of the person concerned.

Our agricultural expert did not 'fail' any more than the children who 'didn't say a word'. It would be more accurate to say that he had made sense of the problem within the conceptual framework

54

provided by his experience of European agriculture: that is to say, he had built a set of constructs relevant to problem-solving in the field of crop cultivation. What had happened was that he then made use of this set of constructs 'beyond their range of convenience', and with correspondingly disastrous results. Had the agriculturalist had the kind of information now available in Europe about local variations in unfamiliar climatic regimes, he might well have modified his set of constructs to accommodate this information: in the absence of such information, however, he could only use what was available to him, his own experience of mid-latitude agriculture. Obviously, we need to distinguish between a possible deficiency in the information available to the construct maker and any conceptual limitations in the ability of the construct maker.

What we are concerned with at this point, however, is just such deficiencies in the information available and their effects upon our ability to build for ourselves a set of constructs that meet the needs of the case. Considered from this point of view, we may better understand the mediaeval natural philosophers when they argued that the sun moved round the earth, for the information which would have led to the modification of this construct had been lost in the centuries following the break-up of the Roman Empire and did not again become available till the end of the fifteenth century. Similarly, it would be somewhat unfair to blame a hill farmer who, finding a fell-walker suffering from exposure, brings him into a warm room and gives him hot drinks or a hot bath. Only recently has research into diathermia shown that this common treatment for exposure can be fatal and that a more appropriate course of action is, in fact, to put the unfortunate person into a bath containing water only one degree higher than the exposed person's body temperature. In severe cases, this may mean that the 'bath' has to be stone cold!

By using his language both to observe and to record and to classify all that goes on around him, a human being develops a way of looking at the world that is intimately related to his own particular experiences. When he encounters new situations, he draws upon his stored experience in order to interpret them. Sometimes his experience is of such a kind that the new situation can be read in the same way as familiar old situations, but sometimes this is not the case. Then we get the mis-readings whose results range from the merely amusing or embarrassing to the unfortunate or even the quite disastrous. Into this first category comes the following story told me by my driving instructor. On one occasion he was proceeding along a quiet road with a pupil whom he considered fairly competent. A roundabout appeared in the distance, so he said, 'When you get to the roundabout, go straight across'. It was fortunate that the roundabout was only about six inches high, for that is exactly what the pupil did. Her 'mistake' was based on the fact that 'straight across' in the past had been confined to crossing roads, not roundabouts. A further factor may have been that she was employing a construct such as 'Instructors say what they mean' or 'Instructors must know what they are doing'.

Unfortunately, misreadings of this kind are often far from amusing and recently a number of tragic accidents, which have made headlines in British newspapers, have pointed to the very high possibility of human misreading as their most likely cause. In June 1972, a Trident aircraft crashed at Staines killing 118 people on board. The lengthy public enquiry which followed this crash established clearly the technical causes of the crash, in this case the premature retraction of the wing leading droops, but what the enquiry was unable to establish was why a number of safety precautions were overridden by the crew and why appropriate recovery procedures were not mobilised in time to prevent the crash. The report suggests that in fact the crew did not 'read' the seriousness of their position. In particular it suggests that the Second Officer whose task was to monitor speed must have assumed that the pilot knew what he was doing. This was a reasonable assumption, given that the Captain was a very experienced pilot, *but* on this occasion the pilot was suffering from an abnormal heart condition which was causing a lack of concentration and impaired judgment. So often did the possibility of mis-reading, rather than mechanical failure, arise in the course of the enquiry that it is not surprising to find among the recommendations made in the report the installation of cockpit voice recorders. What a playback of a cockpit tape from this crash might well have revealed is why no member of the crew read any of the many warning signs that something was amiss and whether, as suggested at the enquiry, there may have been a misreading relatively similar to the pupil's misreading of the driving instructor's 'Go straight across'.

When we consider how easily such situations as these can occur within our own culture it is not surprising that very serious misreadings can occur when we are dealing with the assumptions, attitudes and values of a culture very different from our own, should people continue to read the new situation in terms of what they are already familiar with.

Reading the new in terms of the old is a theme which we shall want to return to in both of the subsequent chapters, particularly when we want to consider the difficulties children may encounter at school, because their reading of the school situation is based on an experience of a community that does not necessarily share a common culture with that of the school. For the moment we must end this chapter by explaining why it is that we lay such an emphasis on the way we read situations, particularly new situations. This, then, is the subject of the final section.

3. 'Seeing' in a changing world

In another context one of the present writers sums up an account of the possible future for the children in our schools in the 1970's by saying that:

'The very least that we can say is that the world in which they celebrate their 65th birthday, the world of the 2020's, will be even more unlike our own world than our own world is unlike the world of 1900. What has happened is that the rate of change has increased out of all proportion to anything men have known in earlier periods. It has reached a point where change grows upon itself, so that we are creating a society in which the *normal* state of that society is one of change.'

Language Study, the teacher and the learner

If we accept that 'we are creating a society in which the *normal* state of that society is one of change', then one might consider what this implies for an individual who has a strong potential tendency to interpret his experience of the world by reading new situations in terms of old. When change was infrequent and very much confined to the sort of changes in the life history of the individual, such as birth, marriage, death, change of activity or occupation, for which an appropriate and public recognised ritual could be provided, then individuals were both alerted to significant change in their lives and helped to come to terms with it by the collective expression of 'the habits of the tribe'. A special effort could be made to 'adjust', and, the adjustment having been made, life could 'go back to normal' in the sense that special effort was no longer required. This was particularly easy to do when the community in which one was having to adjust to change in one's own life did not itself appear to change. Events that did change the life of the community, such as war, plague, or the devastations of natural disasters, were, by definition, not 'change', but aberrations, 'acts of God', discontinuities in the accepted order of things. But what happens, then, when change is not merely personal, but involves the community as well as the individual and is continuous against a background of change. What kind of demand will this put upon the resources of the individual? How can he meet them and what would happen if he fails to do so?

Let us begin by translating this idea of a situation of continuous change into the terms we have been using in this chapter to describe how individual human beings cope with their experience of the world. For the individual we can say that this situation puts him in a position where he is faced with a continuous need to perform his problem-solving in contexts and situations that are marginally or wholly new to him. Now, we have implied that his major resource for interpreting new situations lies in his ability to bring language to bear upon the problems of interpretation they present to him. In particular, by using language in interaction with ourselves, by 'talking to ourselves', exploring the problem inside our own heads, we can think through and test against our previous experience possible solutions. One of the best examples of this is the way we 'rehearse' in our heads, perhaps for days, a difficult letter we are required to write. By using language in interaction with others, however, we can consult with them: we can seek further information and we can use the printed page to extend our own resources. Our capacity to solve our problems, therefore, is directly linked to our capacity to bring language to bear upon them; and our capacity to use language is a function of our experience of using language, an experience immediately relatable to the ways of using language, the attitudes towards, and assumptions about, its use current in our own community.

Consider, for example, the implication of the following comment, made by a man of twenty-seven, a mature student at a College of Education:

'When I first came to College I thought everyone was picking on me. I would say what I thought was right and they would say "No, it's not like that", and then tell me a whole lot of things that I hadn't known about. Sometimes I just said nothing more. Sometimes I lost my temper and just said the first thing that came into my head, usually nasty. But then I began to see that people were still friendly after these arguments and I realised that you

58

could disagree with a person's argument without disagreeing with them as a person. I saw too that even if you thought talking about something got you nowhere, somehow it seemed clearer to you afterwards, even if you still thought the same thing.'

This student read the situation at college in terms of his previous experience. He saw fellow students and lecturers as 'picking on him', because they did not immediately accept the truth of what he said. As this man came from the kind of close-knit community where everyone held the same views on many of the key matters of life, comment in that community would be by definition hostile, for, if it were not, then comment as such would not have been necessary. All that would be required would be a gesture or a word of confirmation. Coming to college, this student reads the presenting of an alternative view as an attack upon himself as it would most certainly have been in his own community had he presented a view different from the one expected of him in the circumstances. It is only because he recognises the friendliness of people, following what he has construed as 'an attack', that he questions his first reading of the situation and, as a result, replaces the construct 'To disagree with what I say is to attack me personally', by the construct, 'To disagree with what I say is to offer an alternative view of the case'. The reader will see that when this student stops using 'picking on me' and starts talking about 'arguing with me', he is not 'being euphemistic', 'speaking properly', or 'talking posh'. Although his contemporaries in his own community might describe his changed behaviour in these terms, he is in fact revealing a basic change in his construct system by his choice of this alternative mode of expression. He does not forget the words 'picking on me', nor does he abandon the construct which guides his use of them. As they no longer fit his view of what happens in his new environment, however, we could say that he has learnt the limits of the range of convenience of the construct concerned and has developed an additional construct to cope with his altered reading of the situation.

The student also makes the point that he used to think 'talking about it got you nowhere'. Most readers of this book will have used talk both personally and professionally to think through their problems, but for this student the idea that talk achieved something was quite new. Having decided that this was the case, however, he was forced to reconsider the relationship between language and action. Like many others in our society, his own community held firmly to the view that language does not, of itself, constitute action. Consider how many phrases in the common language express an underlying sense that language is somehow unrelatable to what actually happens in our own experience. Many of us believe that 'Talking gets you nowhere', or dismiss some comment as 'mere talk', or insist that what is needed is 'Action, not words', or declare that 'There's no good to be done in talking about it'. Perhaps it is fair to say that our student's new experience now puts him in a better position to see what Malinowski really meant when he said that: 'Words are part of actions and they are equivalent to action.' He would also probably be able to see why it is that the writers of this book regard the 'words' used by the two mothers in Chapter 2, as 'actions', actions which have a very powerful effect in shaping events.

This student's view of the world was clearly reflected in his habitual way of speaking. As he changed his way of looking at the world, so he had to find a new way of speaking to express both to himself and to others the new meanings he had made. At the same time, finding this new way of speaking alerted him to new possibilities and prompted him to reconsider other ways of speaking and ways of seeing which he had previously considered 'natural', or 'obvious', and therefore no subject for serious enquiry.

If we accept that the world we live in is in a state of continuous change, change which is unlikely to lessen as time goes on; and if we accept that the ability to utilise the resources of our language in order to make sense of the world and our relationships with other people is our major resource for coping with the problems this situation will create for us; then it would seem to us that understanding how we use language to live is a necessary part of the equipment of every adult and, consequently, the special responsibility of all of us who are concerned with the education of both children and adults in this ever more demanding world.

4 Language in community and school

In the first three chapters of this book we have tried to build up a picture of the way in which the young human being learns to make sense of the world and, in the process, learns both a language and a culture. This complex three-way process brings our child into a specific relationship with the human environment about him, that is, with his community. Providing a child has had continuous contact with such a human environment, by the age of four or five he will have mastered the rules and meanings that make up his language and he will have worked out concretely the rules and meanings that make up the culture of his community. Together, these two sets of rules and meanings, intimately inter-connected as they are, and grounded in his cumulative experience of the world, provide him with a set of constructs that he uses to interpret the continuous inflow of experience which he encounters in his life as a normal human being. What he has achieved in these early years of life is a massive organisation of information about the world. How this organisation is carried out is something that we can only make reasonable guesses at in the present state of our knowledge. What we can be certain about, however, is that it has taken place. There is no other way in which we can account for the enormous success with which the five-year old functions in relation both to the immediate world of its experience and in its use of language in interaction with others. We can also say something about the information itself, what it is that the child organises in those early years, because the substance of much of this information about the world is provided by the language and culture of the child's own community. We may be uncertain as to *how* the child actually acquires the rules and meanings concerned, but we can point to *what* these rules and meanings look like in terms

61

of their practical realisation in the linguistic and social behaviour of communities.

We have now reached the point in our argument where, for the first time in normal circumstances, a child will move outside its community of birth in those countries with a formal education system. By 'going to school' a child enters a new community, and necessarily he is exposed to new ways of seeing, new and different information about the world, new ways of using language and all the unknown situations of a new culture. To some readers, this may seem too extreme a statement, an over-dramatised view of what is a perfectly 'natural' step in the life of every individual. We would ask those readers to suspend judgment for a little and accept that a very strong statement of this kind is necessary just where we do face a situation that so many of us have come to regard as 'natural'. It was not always so, even in our society, as the records of the fierce resistance to compulsory schooling show, and it is not so even now for rather more children in our society than perhaps we are ready to admit. What this chapter is concerned with, therefore, is the justification for so strong a statement about the impact of school upon the child coming new to it.

1. The relationship between school and community

Those readers who are uneasy about the idea that a child moves outside its community of birth for the first time in going to school may have in mind the children who go to the village school, or the children who go to school at the end of their own street, or on their own housing estate. In Britain, at any rate, only a small proportion of primary age children travel long distances to school, in rural areas where schools are not available or in urban areas where parental choice of a particular school make a journey necessary. The point we would make, however, is that geographical distance is not the most important criterion for assessing a change of community. If community is based on shared values, then what we must look at is not the geographical distance between the child's home and the child's school, but the experiential distance between the attitudes and assumptions familiar to the child in his home and those attitudes and assumptions which he will meet in school.

It would seem likely that a child going to a local school, taught by teachers who have been born in the home area, would find

62

them offering him a very similar view of the world to his own, but we have to ask if this would necessarily be so. Firstly, it is unlikely that the child will find 'local' teachers in his school. Teachers are a highly mobile group who work away from their home areas for many reasons. Many infant and junior teachers are married women who move around the country as their husbands move. Another large group of teachers travel away from their home area in order to do the particular work in teaching that appeals to them. A new factor, which has recently contributed to this mobility, is the variation in house prices across the country. The steady outflow of young teachers from the very high-cost areas of London is causing great concern to the local education authorities. The recruitment of more experienced teachers to these areas is also proving increasingly more difficult for the same reason. What these three commonplace factors indicate is the degree to which we are becoming a society where movement is normal and the person who grows up, lives and works in the same locality becomes the exception.

Nevertheless, there are schools where many of the staff are themselves products of the same community as the children they teach. Yet can these staff be said to be 'local' when the cars in the school car-park and the address list in the school office indicate that few, if any, actually live in the area immediately adjacent to the school? This is not an argument for saying that 'teachers ought to live where their pupils live'; it is simply an observation of what seems to be the case for the majority of schools where the writers have either worked or visited. The reason is not mysterious. For social and economic reasons the majority of teachers do not choose to live where their pupils live. Often, indeed, they could not do so even if they wanted to, for few teachers are eligible for the council houses and flats which house a large proportion of Britain's school children.

Beyond all this, however, there is the unavoidable fact that the majority of those who become teachers are changed in the process. They no longer find that they can identify with the values, the attitudes and assumptions, of the pupils they teach, even though those pupils may well be the children of men and women they grew up with.

The reasons for such a radical change in one's view of the world as this are many and complex, but what stands out is the effect of a divergent choice of occupation upon our sense of shared values. At the age of sixteen, the would-be teacher chooses, first, to stay on at school for two years to take A-level and then to continue in full-time formal education for another three or four years. Meanwhile, his contemporaries from his own local community choose to leave at sixteen, take whatever job is available, or go into a job where any further education was in relation to a trade or skill, set in the context of industry or commerce. From his first decision to stay on at school, the teacher no longer leads the same life as his contemporaries, so it becomes increasingly unlikely that he will continue to share their values, even if he believes that he does. This is the case whether his friends work on the shop floors of industrial estates, in the offices of the city centre, or function as executives in any business or industry in Britain. Simply by choosing to become a teacher an individual exposes himself to experiences which are not shareable with his contemporaries. This is also true for doctors or nurses or accountants or surveyors, but the special position of the teacher means that the values he embodies in his view of the world are quite crucial for the basis of his work as a teacher is an assessment of the needs of others, his pupils. If we are to understand how conflict arises in this situation we must first of all see why it is that the teacher so often presents to the pupil, whatever his geographical proximity, or however sympathetic the relationship, a set of values that differ from those the pupil has already developed in the context of his family and his community.

This point has been made at some length, not only because it is important to see that pupils are most likely to encounter different values when they go to school, but also because most readers of this book will be familiar with the arguments put forward in Britain in the last ten years which would explain conflict between pupils and teachers as the expression of a clash between the 'middle-class' values of the teacher and the 'working-class' values of the pupils. This is a very large topic and one which we cannot develop in this present volume, but two points at least must be made. Firstly, it would seem from the ideas implicit in these arguments that there are two, and only two, sets of values at issue; and that the superior virtues of 'working-class', as opposed to 'middle-class' values is self-evident. Secondly, it would seem that these two sets are completely separate from, and diametrically opposed to, each other. It is difficult indeed to accommodate such a view with what we know about the way communities function. If the reader considers the variety of community with which he is familiar, and the success with which communities perform the initial task of socialising their newcomers, then it does seem that adopting a crude dichotomy between middle-class/working class is likely to obscure many of our problems rather than help us to make sense of them by looking at both teachers and pupils in terms of their respective experiences, amongst which their experience of, or sense of, 'class' is certainly very important. If we insist upon a simple two-term system for describing the shared experience of over fifty million people we may indeed be guilty of over-simplification in the cause of ideology.

Let us consider for a moment, a single example of a 'conflict-producing value', one which is shared by all teachers regardless of how they might choose to identify with the values of a particular social class. Most teachers feel that they have 'a responsibility towards their pupils'; that they have some specific role to play in their pupil's development; that when they go into a classroom, they are there to 'do' something. Now this view of the teacher's role finds its realisation in patterns of class-room activity that differ very widely from teacher to teacher. It is realised in one way by the teacher who said to us, 'After all's said and done, they don't know anything until I teach them it, now do they?' and then instructed his student teacher to 'Ram some grammar into them'. It is realised quite differently by the teacher who said, 'Well, it's our job to turn them out able to do a good day's work isn't it?'; or the teacher who said to me, 'We must start where the pupil is and lead him on from there'. Even the teacher who said, 'I just want to create an environment where each individual child can find himself', is offering a version of this role.

Now these four teachers are saying very different things; and indeed, they are very different people with quite diametrically opposed views as to how pupils learn and how, therefore, they should be taught. They have one thing in common, however, They are all committed to changing their pupils. They want to move them from where they are now to a somewhere that they judge their pupils must be in the future. At one level, there is no difference between the objective of the first teacher, who sees 'ramming some grammar into them' as one step towards making them less ignorant; and the objective of the fourth teacher, who wants to exert change through creating an environment where pupils will move from the state they are in at present to a different state, one of 'finding himself', a notion the pupil probably does not have, until this teacher gives it to him. What matters, therefore, is not whether these teachers and their pupils are 'middle-class' or 'working-class', but whether the idea of 'changing', to which all teachers are committed, is understood by their pupils and accepted as one consequence of being at school. Certainly, given what we know about their internal organisation, it is possible that pupils from 'working-class' communities may be more resistant to the idea of 'changing' as such, and less open to the idea that this might be a consequence of going to school, than pupils from 'middle-class' communities. There are very many possible reasons why a human being cannot, will not, dare not, or simply does not want to, change from the position where he or she is at one moment in time to the point where we would like him to be. Because this is the case, we must turn aside from the main theme of this chapter, so that we can look more closely at 'change' in biological and psychological terms before returning to our school-going pupil.

2. A necessary digression

'The key to understanding the significance of the activities of plants, mammals, and men is the recognition of their homeostatic nature, and the fact that they tend to preserve the continuity of life.'

J. Z. Young

'A person anticipates events by construing their replications.'

George Kelly

These two quotations, one from a biologist, one from a psychologist, give us our point of departure, for they remind us of the fact that there are many ways of looking at man, each one of which may add something valuable to the total picture we are interested in building. No one of us can ever experience all the possible ways of looking or seeing for ourselves but we can make use of the 'seeing' of others by testing them out against our own experience of the world. This is what we shall try to do with these two ways of seeing.

In 1932 the word 'homeostasis' was used for the first time. It was used by a physiologist who was writing about a tendency observed in mammals to maintain constant the composition of their blood in spite of changes in their environment. 'Homeostasis' means literally a 'steady standing', a state of equilibrium

66

or balance relative to the surrounding environment. Its importance for our argument derives from the fact that, since the concept was formed in 1932, it has been used and tested by biologists and found to hold good for so many circumstances in the life of organisms, from plants to man, that they are prepared to affirm it as a fundamental organising principle of life itself. Related specifically to man, the concept of homeostasis allows us to suggest that man is designed to keep himself in a state of balance with his immediate environment, and that this involves, not only a balance in terms of his function as a living organism, like his need to keep constant the composition of his own blood, but also in terms of his existence as a social and cultural being, a thinking self.

Contrary to one popular view of their activities, many contemporary biologists do concern themselves with all those aspects of men which to us, as men, seem overwhelmingly important. Though they may find in their work little to support traditional distinctions between 'mind' and 'body', or 'reason' and 'emotion', their view of man does not exclude the behaviour which we associate with our use of these words. What they offer us is a view of man that embraces both his biological continuity with all other living things, and his distinctiveness as a species which has learnt how to emancipate itself from subjection to the constraints of the natural environment by using its brain to create its own environment. In other words, what makes man man is the fact that he has created for himself a social and cultural context which is, for him, his 'natural' environment, that is to say, the environment without which he cannot survive as an individual or as a species. If we now relate the fundamental notion of homeostasis to man as a species whose 'natural' environment is social and cultural, then we can suggest that the individual maintains himself in equilibrium through his control over his relationship to that social and cultural environment.

If, then, we accept that man is unique as a species in that the principle of homeostasis means for him both continuous monitoring of his relationship to the natural environment and to the made environment of society and culture, we can ask what this might imply for him once that made environment was subject to radical change.

Firstly, it might be more accurate if we said that *man must make those adjustments necessary to ensure his own homeostasis*, rather than saying that man changed, or did not change. Now these 'adjustments' could be described in a variety of ways. Depending on one's own personal reading of the situation, they might appear as change, or as resistance to change. Whatever our own personal view of the case, however, we must realise that the adjustment the individual does make is necessary *to him* at the time when he makes it. It is not that he is doing what he *wants* to do necessarily, but what he sees he *has* to do if he is to maintain in equilibrium his relationship to the world about him. He has to maintain himself, because if he does not, he is put at risk. We might say 'he has to be able to live with himself', or 'he has to learn to live with it', or 'he has to come to terms with it'. Perhaps we are very conscious now in our own times that the consequences of failure can be so severe that they destroy the individual concerned.

Let us try to give an example of what we mean by this. A divorced woman has an only son of whom she is extremely proud. She boasts of his doings to her neighbours, telling them how intelligent he is and what her hopes are for him when he grows up. When the child goes to school, difficulties arise. The child seems unable to cope with learning to read and write and the school suggests that special help may be needed. The mother refuses. She is convinced that her son is being misunderstood by his teachers and that his inability to cope with reading and writing is due to his unhappiness with their treatment of him. She continues to refuse special help for her child and continues to tell her neighbours stories about her son's achievements. It is obvious to everyone, except the mother, that the child is in difficulties and needs help, but the mother cannot see this. Some people might say she was 'blind', some 'stupid', some 'neurotic'. What view they took would depend on a variety of circumstances, but in terms of homeostasis, we might say that this mother had made the adjustments necessary to her to maintain her equilibrium. Because of her emotional dependence on her son, she could not face up to the fact that his ability would not fulfill her predictions. In particular, she may not have been able to cope with the imagined reactions of the neighbours to whom she had formerly boasted. It was essential to this woman's well-being that she did not change her view of her son, for changing her view of him meant a whole range of other changes she could not face up to. It was therefore necessary to her to adjust her view of her son's teachers or of his school.

The question of how human beings maintain their steady

state in an environment of change is an important one, particularly if the reader accepts the argument that all teachers are committed to creating an environment in which their pupils are asked
to change.

Let us now relate what we have been saying about the
individual's need to be in equilibrium with his total environment
to what we said in Section 1 of Chapter 3 about the individual's
use of his construct system to, '. . . anticipate events by construing their replication'. As the argument proceeds, we want
the reader to remember the implications of what we have just
said about the class-room and the school as an environment in
which change is continuously demanded of the pupil, because the
substance of what he is asked to do there involves so much that
is necessarily new to his experience. We would also point out that
this newness extends from mental processes to social relationships.

It seems to us that what the biologist, Young, describes as the
individual human being's commitment to maintaining a steady
state in relation to his physical, his social and his cultural
environment, the psychologist, Kelly, describes as the individual
human being seeking always to anticipate events by predicting
that they are about to happen once more, exactly as they have
been known to happen before. If we do indeed cope with our
experience of the world by assuming that it will continue to take
the form that we expect it to take, then we have to accept that,
ordinarily, we go about our daily business of living with a very
low *expectation of change*. We can draw upon strategies for action,
worked out on previous occasions, continuously and unthinkingly,
because we anticipate that events will replicate themselves, so
that the majority of our responses can be 'automatic'.

We are familiar enough with such patterns of 'automatic'
behaviour in our command of commonplace activities like riding
a bicycle, driving a car, knitting a sweater, or playing a game of
tennis. Let us go one stage further, however. How many of us
who drive have a 'normal' route out of our district and how
many of us, on some occasion, have found ourselves happily
driving along this 'normal' route when our journey on this
occasion really required us to set off in the opposite direction?
Similarly, how many of us, after some domestic rearrangement,
say, of books or tools or kitchen equipment find ourselves, for
days, reaching to the old place, the former home of dictionary,
screwdriver or wooden spoon? The next stage is to consider how
often we have gone to take a third or fourth form in September,

69

expecting them to offer a particular pattern of 'difficult' behaviour, even though this form will be composed of between thirty and forty individual pupils who have never been third or fourth formers before? Perhaps the fact that they do so often oblige by giving us the behaviour we predict of them might lead us to ask what part our predictions play in eliciting such behaviour, and what part the local 'habits of the tribe' passed down from one generation of pupils to the next. What we are suggesting then is that the events of our normal day, the routine of rising, the journeys to and from work, the activities of the working day, including even a high proportion of those acts we consciously describe as decisions, we cope with according to well-tested routines.

From both a biological and a psychological point of view, then, we are indeed designed to be, and operate best as, 'creatures of habit'. Were we not so, we would not be able to cope with the sheer volume of continuous problem-solving our encounter with the world thrusts upon us every moment of our working lives. Imagine for example what it would be like if driving to work took as much effort as the very first drives one did when learning to drive, or imagine how the morning schedule would be affected if shaving or making up were not a well-tested routine. In order to cope the better with our immediate and accustomed environment, moreover, very many of the constructs we build have this 'limited range of convenience'. One could say that, in maintaining our steady state successfully, we lose efficiency if we see too many sides of the case. It is interesting to consider how well some familiar aspects of contemporary society recognise this fact. Liam Hudson has suggested that those do best in examinations like the traditional O-level who see only a limited range of possibilities in a question: many firms in the 1960's discovered that graduates were often slower to reach decisions than non-graduates, because they took account of a much wider range of circumstances in the process.

So we come now to the ordinary child, the pupil in front of us, an individual human being who has learnt how to maintain himself in a steady state with his total environment; who has built up a system of personal constructs in the process to enable him to interpret his immediate experience, an experience largely shaped by the social and cultural life of a particular community; and a high proportion of whose existing constructs, therefore, are likely to have a 'limited range of convenience'. What now

70

happens when he comes into this new environment of the school? How is he to maintain himself in equilibrium by adjusting to this new social and cultural environment? What does he do when he has to operate outside the range of convenience of so many of his constructs? Part of the answer is that constructs can be modified, though this takes time, often a very long time. Part of the answer is that it is more efficient for a human being to be able to use initially the constructs it has whatever the immediate consequences of their limited range of convenience than to try to develop a large number of new constructs all at once. As we build our constructs by testing our predictions against real events, we have to be able to experience the *falsification of our predictions*, not once only, but often many times, before we can accept a modification to the construct concerned. There is a sense in which it is proper to say that a construct has to fail before it can be modified. As the construct system is a vital part of the individual human being, however, every prediction falsified by events is a threat to his homeostasis. He must adjust to the new situation to survive, but how this adjustment is made will depend on how he reads the situation. If he reads the newness of the situation as a total threat to his integrity as a person, he may react very violently or withdraw completely within himself in order to keep that self safe from what he construes as an attack.

For some teachers, perhaps, the idea that what they see as 'lethargy', 'stupidity', 'rowdiness' or 'rudeness' in their pupils could be explained in terms of the way a human being is designed to function, may be difficult to accept, but it may be more profitable in the long run.

3. 'On becoming a pupil'

'Stand up properly when you speak to me—take your hands out of your pockets, don't mumble. What was that? You mustn't tell tales you know. He took what? Your work book. Well what was it doing lying around? You mustn't leave things lying around must you?'

This should sound familiar to the reader, for the similarity with our earlier example is deliberate. Once again we have a young human being in a situation where his behaviour is being regulated by adults. This pupil is being presented with a constant stream of information about how he should stand and how he should speak; what he may say and what he may not say; and what attitudes are appropriate towards his own property. The sociologist would call this process 'secondary socialisation' to distinguish it from the 'primary socialisation' we discussed in Chapter 2, Section 2, and we shall see subsequently the importance of this distinction. One common factor, however, in both primary and secondary socialisation, is the use of language to exercise control over others. Just as it was through the language used by adults that the young child learnt to use language itself and learnt the ways of behaving in use in his community, so it is through the language used by a different set of adults, his teachers, in the different environment of the school that the school-age child meets new ways of behaving, new do's and don'ts.

Up to this point, it may seem that we have talked about socialisation as if it were an inevitable one-way process which leaves the child no option but to accept all the values, attitudes and assumptions presented to it by the adults who regulate its world. This was not our intention, for all readers will be only too familiar with the kind of protest a young child can produce when parental control conflicts with the child's immediate interests. On the other hand, it is fair to say that the younger a child the less real possibility it has for rejecting the values presented to it by the adults who control its environment. Until the point where we start to think of the school-going child and even for the majority of those, perhaps, for long after, we are dealing with children who are likely to be deeply affected by the threat of disapproval. For them, the withdrawal of toys, sweets or playmates is a serious matter: the withdrawal of love, affection and sympathy is a disaster to be avoided at all costs. While the child is so vulnerable protest can rarely be sustained for long, but as the child develops towards the young person this situation inevitably changes. As the child comes to handle its language more competently, so it can express its feelings more clearly. As it meets and talks to other children, visits other homes, compares experiences, it sees the possibility of alternatives. Once a child can see the possibility of alternatives to the view of things it has derived from its experience of primary socialisation, there are aspects of that experience which it is capable of reviewing and thus ultimately changing. It has to be said, however, that some authorities would insist that such changes are only ever concerned with relatively unimportant matters and that we carry the marks of our primary socialisation with us to the grave.

72

Protest in a wide variety of forms, however, is a fundamental response of the individual human being to the pressures exerted upon him by the efforts of others to regulate his behaviour, whether he has only the yells of the new-born child as means or the hardware of the urban guerilla. For this reason, it is not surprising that all communities see protest as a threat, and that they have well-tried and tested ways of bringing the views of the individual into line with the view of the community concerned. The pressure to conform is most clearly seen in very close-knit communities, particularly peasant communities, where a divergent member is even more of a threat than in a loose-knit community because his behaviour will be seen by all and will be read as 'a bad example' by the guardians of the community. During the time I spent working in Western Ireland and in Greece I saw many examples of the very strong pressure which the local community could exert upon an individual member. For example, on one occasion I found that one of the two shopkeepers in a small, nearby village was associating with a married woman. In a strongly Catholic and family-centred community, this was a very serious affair. The community succeeded in breaking up the affair by ceasing to patronise the shop of the offending member who was then forced out of business and had to leave the district in order to find work. While the affair was going on, the woman involved was isolated by the women of the community, but after the departure of the shopkeeper she was accepted back into their circle, partly for the sake of her husband and children, and partly because the departure of the shopkeeper gave the community the opportunity to lay blame on him and so avoid the inconvenience of maintaining sanctions against the woman.

The closer-knit the community, the easier it is for the community to function as one and this isolates the offending individual. The sanctions applied range from extreme physical violence such as the killing of a seducer by an avenging brother, still not uncommon in rural areas of Greece, to a beating up meted out to a young man who is thought to have 'got above himself'. Sanctions can also be economic, as with the shopkeeper, but the most familiar sanction of all, practised at every level of society and in every community, is the demonstration of disapproval through the use of certain ways of speaking, or often, *not* speaking, that anyone who has lived in the community will immediately recognise. This demonstration takes a wide variety

73

of forms from the 'raised eyebrow' or the 'cold shoulder' to the total isolation of 'sending to Coventry'. We could say that the language used in interaction with individuals so disapproved of is emptied of all the elements we use to signal responsiveness to the other as a person. It is as if, linguistically, we chose to treat him as an object, even to the point of talking as if he were not present at all.

Given that human-beings have a great need for companionship and social contact, especially in relation to familiar faces, then social pressure of this kind is perhaps the most powerful pressure of all. It is, therefore, social pressure of this kind which is employed when the value system of a group is threatened by the actions or opinions of a newcomer. What particular actions or opinions a community will see as a threat will obviously depend on the community, but, in general terms, what threatens a community is what it really fears and what it really fears is anything that seems to strike at the cohesiveness which gives it its identity. What it is most likely to fear, therefore, is different ways of seeing, different ways of behaving and, of course, the different ways of speaking that make these underlying differences clear, that is, anything which offers an alternative view to the one it embraces for itself.

Now a school is *not* a community, in the full sense of our definition of chapter two. However, like all institutions with an active life of their own, a school does create for the newcomer the conditions we have described as secondary socialisation. In so far as it does socialise those who enter its life, then we can think of it as a particular kind of community. Indeed, there is a long tradition in this country that values the life of the school as a community above its function in imparting knowledge. What we have said so far in this section about the individual in his own community, therefore, we can now apply to the pupil within the 'community' of the school. He joins an institution with a well-developed set of values, attitudes and assumptions. What happens if he protests at their implications for his own activities? What happens if the school does not like his values, his attitudes and assumptions; or his ways of behaving and his ways of using language?

Where schools differ radically from communities is that schools are socialising individuals *who do already have a value system of their own*. This is why the distinction between primary and secondary socialisation is so very important. A community under-

74

takes the primary socialisation of a member who enters it possessing neither language, nor an organised way of looking at the world, while a school creates the conditions for the secondary socialisation of an individual who already has a language and a culture of his own. Unfortunately some schools and some teachers persist in regarding their pupils as 'empty vessels' or 'blank sheets' wanting only the imparting of particular bodies of information in order that their initial ignorance be transformed into later knowledge. To them, all that is relevant is that pupils are ignorant, until instructed in things which the school values as knowledge. If they fail to learn, the fault lies in them. They remain ignorant, because they do not have the ability to become knowledgeable. Failure of this kind in the context of the community of the school, however, is so often read by the school as a global failure of the pupil *as a person.* His success in living the life of his own community is irrelevant, yet to the individual pupil this success is necessarily the basis of his integrity as a person. If pupils are thus presented with such a clash, a clash one could reasonably call a clash between cultures, or ways of evaluating experience, then it is not all that surprising to find deep conflict between pupil and school, and an often violent rejection of the culture of the school.

From all that we have said about primary and secondary socialisation we must accept that a conflict between alternative cultures is extremely likely to arise when a child goes to school. When we consider the capacity of a child to cope with the world, however, conflicting views are not in themselves a threat. If man is a problem-solving animal, then the divergence between alternative views of the world is 'a problem' which could be resolved by each individual child. It is the child's ability to cope with the conflict of views that he meets which would seem to us of real importance, not the mere occurrence of conflict itself. Ultimately, if a child is unable to work out a solution to a problem of this kind, it experiences a kind of frustration which we may not yet fully understand, but whose results we are only too familiar with in terms of a total rejection of all we try to offer in the class-room. How then can we help the child to resolve problems of this kind when it goes to school? Let us ask first how the child would use its natural capabilities as a well-informed human being to set about the problem for itself. It applies its resources to the problem: the language it already possesses, the ways of seeing it has available, and its previous experience of the

75

world which it can draw upon by using language 'inside its head'. All of this, however, the child brings with him from his life in the community. What a child comes to school with is both a language and a culture, each closely bound up with his experience of the other, but it is this language that he must use for learning to be a pupil and for acquiring the 'language for learning' that the school will use throughout the pupil's years of education.

4 'Language for living' and 'language for learning'

What this section is about is how pupils come to see possibilities for using language in different ways. In order to talk about this, we need to be able to focus on what a pupil already possesses when he comes to school and the kind of development which must take place if school is to be both a profitable and enjoyable experience for him. 'Language for living' and 'language for learning' are two terms which will help us to consider this development.

In the first four chapters of this book we have built up a picture of the ways in which a child learns his language and his culture by becoming part of an already established community. He begins this process at birth with the help of a genetic potential to learn language and a capacity to order experience which enables him, through language, to interpret, evaluate and store all his experiences. By being involved in the life of a family and a community the child realises this potential both to learn language and to order his experience of the world, so that he builds up a system of personal constructs which form the basis of the decisions he makes about people, actions and things. The result of this period of intensive ordering and storing is that by school age, say five years old, a normal child has a good command of his language and can use it in a wide variety of ways in the course of his everyday life. It is to this total capacity for using language in everyday life that we give the label 'language for living'. The name itself reflects the basic idea that without language there can be no community, no shared activity, no shared experience; one might say, indeed, no 'living', in the terms that we understand it.

Now the content of any one child's 'language for living' is something that we could work out, if we had enough information about his community and his immediate surroundings. What we can say about *every* child's 'language for living', however, is that it will be intimately related to the ways of speaking of a particular family and a particular social group. What we have tried to stress throughout this book is that a child can only make use of the ways of speaking that are available to him; and if he lives in a community where children have little scope for meeting new situations, and adults, even parents, have little time or inclination for talking with young children, his repertoire of different ways of using language will be limited. If, similarly, a child has accepted the view of a community which thinks that 'children should be seen and not heard'; or that 'children should speak when they are spoken to', then the child's 'language for living' will be markedly different from that of a child who has been encouraged to talk when he has something to say; or to explain what he has been doing; or to express preferences, or to ask questions.

In most cases, whatever our evaluation of the child's 'language for living', it has proved adequate for his needs in his own community. There are two reasons for this. Firstly, the child's language is learnt in that community; hence it is particularly suited to the needs and interests of that community. Secondly, while a child lives exclusively in his own community, that is, while he is below school age, allowances are made for any difficulties he encounters. When the child goes to school, however, there is a radical change. He enters a world, which will be significantly different from his familiar world of home and community. An enormous demand is made upon his linguistic resources for he has to find new ways of speaking to match the new ways of behaving school requires of him. Moreover, this remains fundamentally true however far we may go to meet him by creating conditions in Nursery and Infant school that reflect continuity with his life outside school.

This social aspect of school in itself severely taxes the capacity of many children, but this is far from being the only demand school makes upon them. Schools, even nursery schools, are places where 'learning' takes place and in order to participate in the activities the school provides the child must use language in ways which fit the needs of these activities. It is most likely that, for the majority of children in this country, these ways of using language will be new, or certainly very different from those habitually used in their life outside school. 'Language for learning' is the label we can use to refer to all those ways of speaking which are required by the activities and processes of formal education, and which may or may not already be a part of a child's 'language for living'.

'Tell me what happened in the story'; 'Tell me about the picture'; 'Why did you paint a picture of a rocket?'

From his earliest days in school, the child is expected to meet a whole series of such linguistic demands. He is being asked to use language in ways in which he may never have used it before and, unlike the situation he found himself in as a young child, where adults expected him to have difficulties, 'because he is only a child', it is often now assumed that he can manage 'if only he tries', because he shows he can use some sorts of language very fluently. Because the child has a good command of 'language for living' in his own community, or in the social context of the school environment, it does not mean that he can necessarily cope with 'language for learning'. Some children, of course, do develop some 'language for learning' as part of the total 'language for living' that they take to school with them. For these children, questioning and explaining and finding out about things have already been part of their experience. They will not need to sit silent, as some infant classes do, when a teacher says, 'Tell me about this picture', for they will know that it is the content of the picture, the objects or the people portrayed in it that is being referred to. They will not, as some children do, decide that there is nothing sayable about pictures apart from whom they belong to.

Whatever the variations in the proportion of the language for learning which children bring to the school context, there is one way of using language for learning that very few children bring with them, the ability to use the written language. Throughout this book we have focused on ways of using spoken language, because we have been speaking of pre-school children, but once we talk of school-going children we must add this new way of using language, a way which is entirely different and separate from any of the ways of using language which have previously been mastered. Apart from a possible request to 'write his name', the vast majority of children never meet a situation in their own family and community where they are expected to come to terms with the writing system. For most children, in fact, 'learning to read and write and do sums' is what you go to school for, because this is the view of the school's function they have derived from parents and community.

What we must now do is to see how a pupil acquires the language for learning required by his new environment. In the course of this discussion we must keep in mind one basic question; 'Why is it that any child who has successfully developed language for living in his family and community finds himself unable to go on to develop language for learning in the context of school and formal education? The 'answer', if one can properly speak of an 'answer' to so complex a question, will lie somewhere in the intimate interrelationship of language, community and school. Just as a pupil may come to school with a set of values that may be seriously different from the set of values he encounters at school, so a pupil may also come to school with an established set of ways of using language. Some, or even all, of these ways may limit, or inhibit, or totally prevent, his developing the ways of speaking, and especially perhaps the ways of writing, which are as essential to his every day life in the context of school, as is his language to his life in the context of his community.

5 Family, community and the idea of 'language-climate'

At the end of chapter four we suggested that if we are to understand how an individual acquires language for learning then we must look again at the language for living he acquires in his own community. There are two reasons for this. Firstly, if human beings have both a tendency to see new situations in terms of old, and also a tendency to resist any change that may affect their homeostasis, then it follows that his initial learning of language will have a very profound affect upon his attitude to any future learning of language that he may have to do. The way in which he learns to use language initially, and the attitudes he develops towards the use of language at that time, will shape his approach to learning other ways of using language, not only in the school context, but throughout adult life. Secondly, the rapidity with which social and cultural change occurs in our world puts a premium upon the individual's capacity to find language for coping with the new, but this capacity can be limited by his view of how he can use language both for living and for learning. For both these reasons, therefore, we must look again at family and community, and ask ourselves how their structure might affect the way in which their members come to view the possible uses of language.

1. 'Personal' and 'positional' families

The two terms 'personal' and 'positional' have been used by sociologists to describe two opposite ways in which families can create for themselves the internal cohesion which gives them separate identity. These terms will help us focus on the fact that families do differ from each other in the way they see their individual members and in the ways in which these individual

80

members relate to each other within the family. In these terms, 'positional' families are those in which individuals relate to each other in terms of their relative positions. Father is father, youngest child is youngest child, and the behaviour expected of each is related to this role and its status. Youngest child may not sit in the chair by the fire, because that is father's chair: father may not bath youngest child, because that is the job of mother. The rights and obligations of each member of the family are clear and unambiguous by demonstration, but reasons for these rights and obligations do not have to be given because they are 'understood'. Things are as they are, because that *is* the way they are: the young child makes his way by being told what he must do or must not do, but he is never told why this is the case. In contrast, in a 'personal' family; members relate to each other as fully differentiated individuals. Children, as well as adults, are seen as individual people, as Jean or George or Mary, not as 'eldest son', or 'youngest girl', or 'baby'. Much of what happens in the family is, therefore, the result of negotiation and common agreement, because it is accepted implicitly that all its members have rights *as individuals*, but there is a corresponding obligation to consider the needs of the other members. If this view of the workings of a family seems hard to grasp, consider for a moment this example. What does it tell us about a family if we hear on the one hand a mother say, 'Stop yer noise, you'll wake yer father', and on the other, 'If you make all that noise you'll wake your father, and that's hardly fair when he's been up all night, now is it?' In the personal family things do not happen automatically, because that is the way they always happen, the needs of the individual and of the group are open to discussion and the young child makes his way by being told what he may and may not do, and *why* he may or may not do it.

Now it might be difficult, indeed impossible, to find any one family that will fit either of the simplified descriptions I have given above, but the great value of these two terms is that they allow us to refer easily to common ways of behaving which we have all observed. We can, in fact, make a kind of scale with 'most positional' families at one extreme end and 'most personal' families at the other end. Perhaps the value of these terms as a way of looking at families can best be demonstrated if the reader will pause for a few moments to reflect upon his own family and to try to decide where on our scale his family might come. There are two ways in which the reader can approach this task: either he can try to remember whether there were clear cut rules and regulations for the ways in which the members of his family were expected to behave, or he can try to remember the ways in which language was used to relate to other members of the family. The reason that *either* of these approaches can help the reader to make his assessment is that 'positional' is strongly associated with one set of ways of using language, and 'personal' with another.

In some of the most positional families, families like those I encountered in the remoter parts of Western Ireland, so much of everyday life is governed by long-established rules of behaviour that a whole range of situations which might cause discussion in the personal family simply do not arise. For example, if the division of domestic duties between males and females is specified by the culture, that is, accepted as wholly given, then there is never any question as to who is to do what, or when it has to be done. Moreover, the language used in these circumstances would involve simple assertion: 'I'll be cutting the top field this morning', or a statement of the expected, 'Five o'clock, time to put the meal on'; or an injunction which assumes knowledge of the appropriate action upon the part of the recipient, as with 'Jenny, its five o'clock', where Jenny, as the youngest girl, knows that is her job, and only her job to lay the table for the evening meal. In the context of the personal family, however, any domestic task might be done by any member of the family who was competent to do it, so that the use of language for considering possibilities, making alternative suggestions, planning what has been agreed, or justifying a particular plan by offering evidence in support of it, would be involved. We must emphasise, however, that what is characterised here is two alternative *styles* of organising one's life, not two absolutely exclusive *modes of using language*. What the *style* of living does is to make the need for one or other *mode of using language* more or less likely.

What we are trying to indicate by using this extreme example of personal and positional families, is that the way a family is organised in terms of who can do and say what things to which people is crucial to the child's understanding of what it can do with language. Clearly, a positional style of organising the life of family or community does limit the options open to the child for finding out what he can do by using language in different ways.

'Don't speak to me like that.'
'Don't answer me back.'
'Do it when I say so and don't ask questions.'

These three commands can be looked at in terms of the relationship between speaker and hearer, or they can be considered in terms of the linguistic options they leave open to the recipient. Possible responses are fairly limited for this particular recipient: he must speak in an acceptable way, acceptable that is, to the controlling adult: he must not offer an alternative view of the case to that presented by this adult, whether or not he knows why he must do so, because he is forbidden to ask questions. One wonders if there is any linguistic alternative at all open to this hearer other than silence. Perhaps, even, this was the intended consequence of the speakers choice of words. In terms of relationship, we could say that instructions such as these are a recurrent feature of the life style of positional families, where there is a strong focus on status, and a sharp dichotomy, therefore, between the relative status of adults and children. It is the sharp distinction between child and adult, between younger and older adult, between male and female, that makes so many ways of speaking unacceptable. It is in this way, therefore, that the pattern of family relationships can directly affect the linguistic options open to its members. If a whole range of linguistic options is closed to a child, it may well be that it includes options which form part of the language for learning that the school requires from the child.

Let us take a specific example. Many teachers in both primary and secondary schools require from their pupils a willingness and an ability to take part in class discussions, to participate in what we can call *exploratory talk*. This kind of talk is familiar to all readers of this book: it occurs whenever a group of people get together to consider a course of action, whether the action is choosing a day's outing, or deciding the content of next term's courses. Exploratory talk is characterised by the opportunity it gives for us to test out half-formed or tentative ideas. Each participant considers the contributions of others and accepts that the object of the talk is to make the best sense of the matter in hand, given the information that is available. Now what is the position of the pupil who has never heard this kind of talk? What is there in his experience that he can draw upon in order to take part in the talk as he is bidden?

We could put this rather differently by asking what constructs he could draw upon to help him solve his problem (see page 50).

If the child comes from a family and a community where he has never heard exploratory talk the range of convenience of the constructs he has formed to help him interpret the use of language face-to-face will be too limited for his present needs. What this limitation looks like and how it affects the reading of a new situation is well illustrated by the following comment, a comment made by a mature student at a College of Education about his own experience.

'When I first came to College what I couldn't stand was all the arguing. The lecturer would stand up and say something and someone would start to argue with him and it would go on and on and I would think, "We're never going to get anything done here". It seemed to me that they were just bickering instead of getting on with it, though the lecturer didn't seem to mind. I suppose really it was because of my father. He couldn't stand arguments. If you ever started to disagree with anything he said, he would just lose his temper and say "I'm telling you, there's no two ways about it", and off he'd go. I suppose when I first came to College I saw discussion as argument. I couldn't see any point in it. After all, the lecturer knew and we didn't, so it was up to him to talk and us to listen.'

This comment, together with the example provided by another student in Chapter 3, page 58, gives us some idea of how exploratory talk must look to the individual who has never experienced this kind of talk before. Some interpretation has to be found for what is going on and if the only constructs available in the individual's experience involve 'picking on me', 'bickering' and 'argument' then these terms will be used, however unfortunate their connotations in the context of exploratory discussion. Later in this chapter we shall look at how these two students came to develop new constructs related to the exploratory talk which they now had access to, but for the moment let us look again at what this student is revealing about the attitudes to language he has acquired in the process of learning his language in the context of his own family.

In his family, the relationship between father and son was such that whatever father said had to be accepted. It is not considered appropriate behaviour for a son to argue with his father. If the father holds the view that 'There are no two ways about' any subject, then the putting forward of *any* alternative view of the case, or any qualification of the position the father has asserted, will be construed as 'argument'. A further element in the student's

84

experience of learning is revealed by his assumption that those who 'know' have a right to speak and those who don't ought to be silent. It is very likely that his father would insist upon his status (a) as male, (b) as father, that is, titular head of the family, (c) as adult, in insisting on the rightness of his views when 'arguing' with his son. His son, therefore, has come to accept a link, on the one hand, between status and 'having the right to speak' and, on the other, between authority and knowledge. That a class of mature students, sharing a wide and rich experience of the world, might indeed 'know more' than their lecturer on many occasions, and that their lecturer might be wise enough to see this, is beyond the range of convenience of the constructs about talking, about knowing and about learning that this student has brought with him from his early experience of these things in the context of his own socialisation.

In this one short comment, this student reveals a great deal about the way language could be used in his family. He also gives some indication of the tightly regulated relationship he has available with his father. What is also revealed is the potential for continuity which the adoption of these particular attitudes to language would give to a family or to a community. If one eliminates the right of an individual to present alternatives by making all exchange of views, all qualification of another's assertions, 'argument'; if one then makes 'argument' a crime against the authority structure of the family and if one denies the right to speak to anyone who does not 'know' what the family or community 'knows', then any change of attitude or assumption within family or community will be very unlikely, except as a very slow process over generations. One result of this kind of structure is that any strong-minded person who insists on his right to advance his own view of things will either leave the community out of frustration, or be forced out by the weight of hostile opinion. Once again, the net result is to reinforce the perpetuation of the 'likemindedness' of the family or community concerned.

We are not asking at this point whether or not continuity of this kind in communities is 'a good thing' or 'a bad thing'. There are consequences, however, for the individual and the community, when society as a whole is no longer organised as a series of such communities. Just as the student who revealed these attitudes to language had difficulties when he encountered a new situation, so communities who perpetuate these attitudes to language will inevitably have difficulties if they encounter new situations. The possibility of there being a community in this country which can avoid new situations as we move towards the end of the century seems to us very unlikely.

2. 'Language climate' in family and community

Let us begin by using an illustration to help us define exactly what it is that we mean by 'language climate'.

Just before we left London to come to Manchester, we received two separate invitations to spend the evening with senior professional colleagues whose homes we had not previously visited. Our only information about the social situation we would meet on these two occasions was that an evening meal would be provided. In the event we met two very different situations. On the first occasion, we were welcomed to an elegantly furnished house where our hostess, wearing a long velvet skirt, talked about the dreadful weather as she led us to a panelled drawing-room where sherry was being served. Through the double doors leading to the dining-room, we could see a polished oval table, with cut glass and cutlery laid for eight people.

On the second occasion, we found that our host lived in a ground floor flat of a large block of flats. He greeted us at his front door wearing an apron which said 'Keep Britain dry' and carrying his two year old son. He apologised for the temporary absence of his wife who was 'having a fight with the oven', and led us to a small sitting-room where a dozen people were sitting or standing in groups talking, and a table was stacked high with plates, cutlery and paper napkins for a buffet supper.

Now both these situations required from the writers the kind of assessment which the reader will have made many, many times for himself, unthinkingly, when faced, as we were, with a new situation where he was required to interact with a group of people more or less unknown to him. The most immediate thing that the reader would do, as we did, was to make an assessment of the formality or informality of the occasion. In any situation one has to prepare a plan of action before speaking, and assessing the formality or informality of the occasion is a first step in making a whole series of further decisions about what actions might or might not be acceptable in this context. Some of these decisions are decisions about the use of language: to talk or not to talk; to initiate conversation or to let others take the lead; to change the topic of conversation; to listen or to remain silent. One might quickly make up one's mind that certain topics were to be avoided or that certain topics would be appropriate. For example, on the first occasion a remark of the hostess about the sad fate of the local selective school suggested that the subject of comprehensive education would not be an appropriate one. All of the decisions, therefore, which the reader might make in a social setting, be it informal or formal, professional or personal, pleasurable or otherwise, are based on his reading of the situation, his assessment of the total 'atmosphere'. It is to that part of the total atmosphere which influences our decisions concerning our use of language that we give the name 'language-climate'.

Every reader will be able to think of his experience of a whole variety of different language climates. Some of these language climates we might describe as 'hostile': for example, the very formal interview where the reader felt unable to use his habitual ways of speaking, but was forced into ways of speaking where he felt uneasy. This was, indeed, the writer's experience at that very formal dinner party. On the other hand, there are 'supportive' language-climates, the kind which one often finds in the company of old friends, or long standing colleagues, where one need not fear being misunderstood and where one can risk revealing a half-formed idea, or make a spontaneous comment.

As with the terms 'positional' and 'personal' we do not want to focus upon 'ideal' examples of either 'hostile' or 'supportive' climates, we want rather to use the terms in order to point to the particular elements in situations which shape our linguistic response to them. The key feature of the language climate as far as the individual speaker is concerned is his freedom or otherwise to use language in the ways in which he is most happy to use language in expressing his view of the world and his relationship to others, 'hostile' and 'supportive' help us to focus upon this key feature.

We can use the example of the informal supper, and the formal dinner, to illustrate some of the distinctive features of 'hostile' and 'supportive' language-climates. We can only compare them, however, if we consider them in respect of an individual who is *equally familiar* with both formal and informal situations of this kind. There is a sense in which the language-climate of *any* situation is likely to be read as hostile by an individual who has no previous experience of similar situations as our student so read the seminar situation at college.

Let us assume then that the reader has experienced occasions similar to the two that we are considering. We can make certain predictions about the linguistic demands which the two evenings would have made upon him. In linguistic terms, the demands of the larger informal gathering in the small sitting-room are far greater than the demands of the formal dinner party. In a setting such as the informal supper party the 'rules' for behaviour, linguistic and otherwise, are more open and flexible than in the formal setting. A great deal more is left to the individual judgment and discretion of the participants. For example, in this situation the reader would have had to decide for himself whether he was entitled to talk to one person all evening because they had found a topic of great mutual interest, or whether he should talk to as many people as possible, restricting himself more or less to social talk in doing so. He will have to decide whether to join in the talk of an existing small group at a particular moment, or whether to wait until the topic under discussion changes. There are also decisions to make as to whether to help with serving supper, whether to offer to help with the washing up, whether to leave when the first guests leave, or whether to stay to the end. This informal situation, by leaving open so many alternative possibilities for action, makes a very great demand upon the individual in selecting from all these possibilities the ones which best relate him to the situation. In meeting this demand, however, the reader would have the freedom to talk or to remain silent, to join a conversation, to change the subject, to assert a point of view, to express his sincerely held convictions, or to ask questions, for the language climate is basically 'supportive'.

At the formal dinner party, the reader would have found very few of these linguistic possibilities open to him. On the other hand, provided that he was familiar with such settings, choice of what to do or say would present very little difficulty just because the options available were so limited. A limited range of options means that linguistic events become highly predictable, so that, once an initial reading of the situation has been made, what follows has little that is 'new' about it. In terms of language climate, therefore, it is proper to say that the formal setting is the more 'hostile', because the only alternative to knowing, and keeping, the rules is silence. We have the seeming paradox, therefore, that the more difficult setting in terms of the demands it makes upon our capacity to language is, in fact, the more 'supportive', while the setting that makes the fewest demands, because it offers virtually no options to the participants, is the more 'hostile'. We can test this by asking ourselves what would be the fate of someone who was equally unfamiliar with both these settings. It is reasonable to suggest that, in the formal setting, he would be virtually excluded from any active participation in the events of the evening, while in the informal setting he would feel able to risk some sort of participation, however tentative, because he would sense that this was one of the options available.

The formality or informality, of relationships would seem to be a key factor in the formation of language climates and indeed the reader may have observed the similarity between what we have said about the language climate of formal and informal settings and what we have said about the relative formality of positional and personal families. For example, in the less strictly regulated personal family individuals generally find they need to use language in a wide variety of ways, and make decisions continuously as to the appropriate thing to say next. In this sense, there is a similarity here with what has been said about the informal supper party. On the other hand, the positional family has a fixed pattern of relationship and correspondingly limited options for using language very similar to the rule-bound nature of the formal dinner party. In the case of both positional family and formal dinner party there are very clear rules governing who can say what to whom and in what manner. The rules are not made explicit, because participants are *expected* to know the rules, and the rules allow only a certain limited range of linguistic options to them.

Once again we must say that it is not our concern to ask whether the limiting of linguistic possibilities is in itself 'a good thing' or 'a bad thing', or what the relationship is between personal and positional families and social structure. What we must ask instead is whether the limiting of linguistic options in the way we have described, and the resulting effect on the individual child, pupil or adult, will enable him to deal more easily or less easily, with the range of situations, familiar and unfamiliar, which he is likely to meet in his everyday life.

So far, we have been talking exclusively about personal and positional families and we have had to point to one key feature of the language climate of the positional family, its limitation on the options it allows its members in their use of language for living. After the age of five, however, a child spends progressively less time exclusively within his own family environment. School becomes a major factor in his life, and friends and playmates provide access to other homes and other families. It might be thought that the child from a positional family would gain access to those ways of speaking which were not part of his own family experience through his contact with other families and with school. The language climate of schools will be the topic of section four of this chapter. What we must do here is to consider the relationship between family and community in terms of their respective language climates.

When we were working towards a definition of community in Chapter 2 we suggested that the most important force in creating communities was the sharing, and perpetuating, of a particular set of values. In particular, we pointed out that factors like geographical proximity were of minor significance in the development of 'us-ness' compared with even the most simple shared value, attitude or assumption. Hence we were led to describe 'positional' and 'personal' as ways of experiencing values, the organising of deeply-held beliefs so that they express themselves in terms of a particular pattern of relationships and a particular pattern of using language. If we find a whole group of families organising their beliefs along similar lines there are two questions we must ask. Firstly, 'Whence came the model for these families to use in organising their beliefs?' If we answer, 'From the community, of course, the repository of the shared values of the culture', then we must ask, 'Is it then reasonable to extend the range of convenience of our terms "positional" and "personal" so that they will refer to the organisation of life within the community as well as within the family?'

These are very difficult questions and anything like a full answer is beyond the scope of this book, but it has to be said that the answers to these questions are far from being of theoretical interest only. From my own fieldwork observations in very different communities, and recent work describing the life of communities in Britain, examined with this perspective in mind, my feeling is that 'positional' in the family is a reflection of 'positional' in the community. If this *is* the case, then the implications are very important indeed, for this means that the child from a positional home is likely to encounter the *same* ways of organising relationships, and the *same* ways of using language, in his dealings with his community, as he experienced in his own family. We could also make the further point, that the more positional a community is,

90

the more intolerant it is of alternative ways of behaving, and hence the more likely that a friendship between a child from a 'positional' family and a child from a 'personal' family will be short-lived.

This leaves the school. What we are likely to find in the schools of a 'positional' community is one of two things. On the one hand, in a fairly small number of cases, there is complete accord between the culture of the community and the culture of the school. so that there is a continuity of language climate between them. On the other hand, in a much larger proportion of schools, there is a gap between the culture of the community and the culture of the school which is so wide that there is a total discontinuity between them. In the first case, the pupil meets little or no opportunity to acquire new ways of using language for living; in the second, he cannot carry home what he finds at school, or use in school what he uses at home. Only the most tough-minded children can tolerate the strain of having to live what amounts to two separate lives. The majority do what one would expect: bow to the ties of home and community and contract out of the culture of the school entirely.

If an individual brought up in a positional family within a positional community spends his life in that community, it would be fair to say that there would be much in his life that he could always take completely for granted. His capacity to construe events by their replication would be very high, because of the relatively limited range of options open to him, and his need to read and interpret new situations would be very low. The language climate of his whole environment would be entirely supportive to him in that only his habitual ways of speaking would be required. What then will happen if the urban area where he lives is declared a slum and clearance begins; or if the mine, or mill, or factory, where he works, closes and there are no alternative jobs in the area, or if a motorway turns his remote village into a commuter's paradise; or if an oil rig turns his fishing village into an oil town; or if industrialised agriculture, reafforestation, or mining, changes the composition of the local population? What happens is that changes will occur that will radically alter the fabric of the community he has known and within which he is able to operate so successfully, and change of this order is the last thing for which the individual from the positional family and positional community is in any way equipped to handle.

3. Change: the role of the language climate

Not all individuals will be in such vulnerable positions as those in the situations we suggested at the end of the last section, but if change is something which will inevitably affect every individual alive in the last quarter of the twentieth century then we may well ask how they are going to cope? Although there are many answers to that question, the reader will be able to supply a range of examples of his own which illustrate the different ways in which people already do cope with change. At one end of the 'coping' scale we have the 'non-copers', the people who simply cannot manage to come to terms with whatever change faces them whether it is social, economic, practical or personal and their unhappy stories reach our newspapers daily.

Another group try to cope with change by pretending that it has not occurred There is the Grammar school headmistress who tries to enforce the wearing of gloves by teenagers in the 1970's; the old man who refuses to believe that the motorway really is going to be built through his condemned house; the parents who cannot accept that their children are now adults. Then there are those people who just manage to cope, who do 'get by' or 'muddle through' or 'manage somehow'. Their coping does not make the newspapers, or even the doctor's surgery, so we seldom have any evidence for the time or energy or anxiety that they have expended in order to come to terms with whatever changes have occurred. At the furthest end of the scale, we have those people who find change presents little problem to them. They 'take things in their stride' and adapt to the new situation without any particular visible stress or anxiety. How do they do it?

The answer to this question is unlikely to be simple, but one element is sure to be involved: the part played in their ability to cope by a highly developed capacity to use language 'on their feet'. Let the reader choose any change that he has ever had to cope with and consider what part language played at every stage in the process. Firstly, language will have entered into his initial reading of the situation; then he will have used language to think through the problems involved. Language comes in when we decide to ask for help from friends, to request or gather factual information, to sort and categorise this new information. If there is no stage in reading, assessing, deciding or acting in order to cope with change that does not use language, either internally or externally, then it would seem that the language we bring to bear upon the task is the key factor in our success or failure.

The language any one of us brings to a situation, however, is a product of our experience and of our opportunity both to observe and to practise ways of using language. We have pointed, too, to the limited ways of seeing and behaving and speaking that are characteristics of the positional family and community. This would lead us to the idea that those people who can best cope with change are those whose experience of using language and making decisions embraces a very wide range of different situations, and has frequently required them to cope with the linguistic demands of situations new to them. It would seem that some people have a much greater capacity to 'work things out for themselves' than others. Perhaps we might be in a better position to ask how this necessary process is best developed or accelerated if we could get a clear idea of what 'working things out for themselves' really looks like.

In the course of writing, I have already used comments made by mature students at a College of Education. These comments were recorded after discussions with students about the changes they had encountered in their lives and how they had coped with them. As the students had indeed 'worked things out for themselves' we can use their comments as a starting point.

'When I first went to Grammar School it was like going into a different world. They even spoke so differently that they wouldn't have understood me if I'd spoken the way we spoke at home. I began to feel terribly inferior, because I couldn't express myself. At home no-one ever said very much. Dad was out all day and Mum had four of us to look after, so there didn't seem much to talk about. Then I found I could do languages. I think it was because they taught you from the beginning, not just expected you to know and I decided I wanted to get away. I saw that if I could do things like the others, I could go on to College, so I started to try to say more. It was awful, but I managed because I knew what I wanted.'

'Before I came to College I lived in Exbury, I went to school in Exbury, I worked in Exbury and I married an Exbury man. I couldn't imagine that people really lived any differently, or thought any differently, from the way that I thought. When I came to College I couldn't get used to being with people from different places especially foreigners. I found I could often get on better with the foreigners than with the people who lived only a few miles away from where I lived myself. I never thought that people who lived so close could think so differently, or people who lived so far away could have such similar ideas about certain things. I realised that if you wanted to understand people you had to find out what they thought, not assume that they thought like you.'

Now the experiences which these three students are recounting are different in detail, but there is a common quality in the experience which they have gone through. All of the students began their lives in a situation which limited their experience of the world. They lived, respectively, in a Manchester industrial suburb of nineteenth century back-to-back houses: in a mining village in North Yorkshire and in a high-cost, low density, garden suburb in Cheshire. All three students considered that their homes were 'more positional', and that all three homes made it clear that their own particular way of behaving was the 'right' and 'obvious' way to behave. But what in fact has happened to the students?

In all three cases, they have encountered a new situation, one with which they were quite unfamiliar and one which presents, not just a different, but often an opposite view to the one they themselves hold. Mr A sees the discussions of his first months at College as 'arguments', when people 'pick on him'. Mrs B finds that at Grammar School you are expected to be able to express what you are thinking, while at home it is considered that 'there isn't much to say'. Mrs C discovers that not everyone in the world thinks like she does. This, however, is not the end of the process, but the beginning, for in each case the students observe the new situation. They read what they see happening in discussion, in the classroom, in contact with new people, and they match it with what is familiar to them in their own construct system. Mr A, for example, matches 'discussion' to 'argument' but in fact rejects his own reading when, as he says himself, he saw 'that people were still friendly after one of these arguments'. He is alerted to the fact that the new situation is different and, having seen this, he moves towards it in order to find out more.

One might say that each student moves towards the new situation rather as one might move towards a nearby hill to view one's former position in the hollow. Like moving to a new physical viewpoint, moving to a new mental viewpoint has two effects: it allows one to view at close quarters a new piece of landscape and it allows one to look back at the point from which one has come.

As one student summed up his experience for me: 'Once you've

94

realised that there is more than one way of looking at anything, then you are never the same again, for when you meet something new, you are on the look out for things, you may not know what, but at least you know to look'.

What in fact the students described to me is a process which was observed and written about at length by G. H. Mead, the social psychologist. He calls this process of moving towards the new and reconsidering what has gone before 'reflexiveness'. He sees it as,

'the turning back of the experience of the individual upon himself'.

He also sees it as a process which enables the individual,

'To take the attitude of the other towards himself'.

We could say that reflexiveness gives us the opportunity BOTH to put ourselves in a different position from the one we have always been accustomed to adopt, so that we can experience that position for ourselves, AND to put ourself in a different position, so that we can review our own experience by standing outside and looking in upon what is familiar and habitual to us. We can demonstrate this process by recording what an individual might be thinking at various stages on his journey from a familiar and known perspective to his taking up a new and unfamiliar one.

'Ah—I thought that was obvious, but it isn't.'
'So that's how it affects me, is it?'
'So that's what it means in my life to . . .'
'So that's what it means in life to . . .'

The ability to be reflexive which these mature students have developed, has helped them to adjust to very considerable changes in their lives. It has also given them the confidence to say that, although they may not *welcome* change, they do feel now that they will be able to 'think it through for themselves' and make the relevant decisions. If reflexiveness is indeed a capacity that can be developed to help individuals cope with change, and if schools accept that part of their job is to equip the individual for coping with his life beyond school, then there are two questions we must ask about schools. Firstly, do schools provide the right kind of opportunities for pupils and students to explore ways of thinking and talking alternative to those which have been habitual to them in family and community? Secondly, do schools provide the supportive language climate which will be necessary if the pupil or student is to have the courage to develop the linguistic competence without which he cannot be reflexive?

It may be that there are as many answers to the first of these questions as there are individual schools. Certainly the reader will be able to supply some answers from his own experience. What we must do in the remaining space we have is to consider what the language climate of schools might look like.

4. The language climate of schools

In the first two sections of this chapter we explored the way in which the organisation of relationships in family and community affects the individual by extending or narrowing the options available to him when he uses language. We then considered the implications of this for an individual who was faced with living in an environment of continuous change. We argued that one key factor was his ability to bring language to bear upon the new experience which confronted him, and we suggested that this was linked with his ability to be reflexive about his experience. We went on to say that this reflexiveness could not be fully developed unless opportunities occurred for the individual to extend both his ways of thinking and his ways of speaking. Extending one's ways of speaking is a complex process, for it must involve exposure to new experience and we have already considered at length what difficulties new experience presents to the majority of people. The language climate is also involved in the process and enough has been said about the language climate of different kinds of community for the reader to see that the process of coming to terms with new experience is actively supported by some climates, while many can be neutral, or even entirely hostile to the process. What we must now consider is the language climate in schools. If we accept that extending an individual's linguistic competence is a necessary objective for the school and if we accept that extending this competence is best pursued in a supportive language climate, then we have to recognise that school is the most likely, or even the *only* possible, source of such a climate for the majority of our children at the present time.

Most readers will have been inside a number of schools, whether as pupils, or subsequently as parents and as teachers. Some readers will have experience of very many schools, because of their professional concerns, but all readers will be aware of the differences that are immediately observable when one goes from one school to another. Some schools have a well-cared for appearance with bright wall displays, flowers and pupils' work

96

carefully arranged: some seem uncared for, cheerless and bleak. From school to school, noise levels vary from the silence of the tomb to the hubbub of the marketplace. In some schools, pupils chatter in corridors; in others, file silently from class-room to class-room. For those who visit schools professionally such small individual features have more than superficial meaning For example, a skilled reader of schools can tell from the rules he observes in practice the attitude of the staff towards the pupils: whether they regard pupils as objects to be organised and controlled, or as individuals with the capacity to think for themselves and to make decisions. He can work out from his reading of the 'atmosphere' of the school some of the underlying attitudes which grow and develop when a group of people interact over a period of time. What we want to focus on particularly is how this atmosphere affects the language climate of the school, and therefore the use of language by all those who work there. We must focus upon the cultural climate of the school as a whole and consider which of its assumptions, attitudes and values most immediately contribute to the creation of its language climate. For example, in terms of language climate, it may not matter whether or not there are flowers in the class-room, but it may be critical that talking is forbidden in corridors.

Let us look now at one of the most accessible parts of the culture of the school, its 'rules'. Consider the following:

'Don't talk in class'
'Don't talk in the hall'
'Don't talk in the corridors'
'Don't speak to a teacher like that'
'Don't answer back'

Once again we ask the reader to reconstruct from his own experience the language climate of any school in which he was a pupil. Hopefully, it will not have been like the hostile climate created by the school where these five rules were in use. In that particular school, the linguistic options presented to pupils were so limited that most pupils had taken refuge in apathy, the behavioural equivalent of silence, or absenteeism. If we look closely at the five rules we see that they circumscribe speech between pupils and between teacher and pupil. The only form of verbal exchange between teacher and pupil was the question and answer form. The reciprocal use of language, as in dialogue proper, was simply 'unthinkable' for teacher or pupil. In many cases, the teacher shaped the sentences and required only the appropriate one word reply slotted in to the appropriate space. The spoken language used in learning was thus confined to one simple kind: the other major form of language use was a brusque language of control, which required only compliance on the part of the pupil, or at best a verbal sign of acquiescence such as, 'Yes, miss'. It is such features of this school language climate as these that make it fair to suggest that we have here a climate closely analogous to the one we have already explored when we discussed positional families.

This is an extreme, but not untypical, example of how a climate is created in which pupils have little opportunity to develop their thinking or ways of expressing themselves. It is not surprising that a personnel manager interviewing pupils from this school should complain that not one boy or girl had been able to say two sentences in reply to his questions without using such fillers as 'You know . . .', 'Kind of . . .' 'like'. We would ask when these boys and girls had last been presented with the opportunity to utter a complete sentence without fear of interruption or criticism.

We must now look beyond such an extreme example as this. There are many, many schools where one might say that the cultural climate as a whole was much less hostile to pupils, but where a close examination of the language climate might reveal serious limitations in its capacity to be supportive.

Consider the following 'rules'

'Don't ask questions now, there may be time later.'
'I'm not interested in the experiment being exciting: we only want results and diagrams.'
'Don't sit there reading, you're supposed to be outside.'
'Comics and other magazines must not be brought into school.'
'Juniors always play this side: the Seniors go over there.'

While considerably less abrasive than our first set of rules, these are equally limiting in their effect upon the linguistic options pupils will feel they are able to take up in the environment of the school. They also remind us that if we want to see the full extent of the features which go to make up a language climate we must look in the corridors and in the playground as well as in the classrooms. We should consider what possibilities are open to pupils when they are not in class, but still within the school. What would the reader now make of the following unwritten rule, 'Girls are not permitted to use the Library on dry days', or the injunction of one headmaster to his younger staff that they should not 'fraternise with pupils on the school premises' as this would 'undermine

98

discipline'; or of another that pupils should be discouraged from discussing their school work with their parents.

Let us consider for a moment what the effect might be on a pupil from a 'more positional' family who comes to a school where the language climate is hostile. In his family and community, this pupil will have acquired a set of ideas about what can be done with language. He will be familiar with the idea of language as a means of social control: he is controlled by his parents or elders; in turn he controls younger children by using the same forms. He has developed a 'language for living' which he uses to carry on his life as brother, son, boy-next-door, friend, member of a peer group. In a hostile language climate, he will meet a language of control that is certainly familiar to him in one sense, for it will be peremptory and will not be explicit as to the reasons for its commands. However, it will be exerted, not by members of his own community, but by 'outsiders', outsiders who are putting pressure upon him at the same time to use a 'language for learning' that he has little opportunity to acquire as they do not offer the opportunity to practice. Not surprisingly, this pupil is unwilling to 'get it wrong', by trying a half-formed sentence with a teacher who is likely to say, 'Come along, boy, out with it, I can't stay here all day.'

At the same time, we can ask what opportunity this pupil will have for seeing language used in new ways, ways that are different from any that he knows from his home situation, other than those that are least accessible to him, the ways of using language for learning customary in the context of formal education. Given such a climate, he may well leave school, as the student quoted on page 84, without ever having taken part in discussion, without ever having been asked to consider, to select, to report, to plan or to argue. Far from presenting alternatives his time at school will have offered him only what he was already familiar with, and offered it in such a way as to alienate and antagonise him. On the other hand, were the pupil to find himself in one of the many schools where staff have given their attention to creating conditions in which pupils feel secure and able to 'risk' the hazard of speaking about what they 'don't know', are 'not sure of', or 'have had an idea about', then he would be in a totally different position. In this climate, a condition which we find in many of the best primary schools, particularly those where the teachers have constant contact with each other and a deep knowledge of the community from which their pupils come, our pupil would see and hear pupils and teachers engaging in a kind of talk that he had not experienced at home. By sharing in the activities of the class, he could enter into the talk, at first tentatively, and then more confidently, until ultimately he had added to his ways of speaking the ability to discuss, to plan, to imagine, to speculate and to share all this both with his peers and with his teachers.

From the foregoing, it is clear that a key difference between the hostile and the supportive language climate lies in the relationships which are possible between staff and pupils. The hostile climate is likely to be found where staff/pupil boundaries are strictly maintained:

'Staff corridor—no admission.'
'Say "Sir", when you speak to me.'

A supportive climate is much more likely to be found where staff/pupil relations are friendly and less formal:

'How would you describe that shape? Anyone got any ideas?'
'Can someone help me with the projector?'

This contrast is not accidental. Formality is a device used in most human communities to limit the terms of some relationships, and to exclude others as 'unthinkable'. Like many other such devices formality makes life much easier for all who participate in those relationships. 'You know where you are', in relation to anyone met with in the community: that is to say, the degree of intimacy is pre-established and what can, and cannot, be a part of the relationship is determined by the degree of intimacy involved. On the other hand, informality allows very wide variations of behaviour within the bounds of a particular relationship. Formality makes predicting future responses very easy: informality requires that we monitor closely the progress of the interaction all the time. For some teachers and some schools, this degree of indeterminacy in the relationship between teacher and pupil is quite unacceptable. The Headmaster who did not want his staff to 'fraternise' with their pupils was no fool: intuitively, he realised that a change in the degree of formality means a change in the terms of the interaction between staff and pupils. Change of this kind is something which neither party may wish to cope with, because it involves the learning of new ways of behaving and new ways of languaging. As this headmaster realised, in the context of a school, new ways of behaving imply new ways of controlling others. A change in the language climate of a school necessarily implies some change in that part of the cultural climate of the school concerned with maintaining 'good order and discipline'. 5547 73

At this point it is necessary to say again that pupils as much as teachers may resist any change that seems to require an effort from them. For the writer's however, the teacher's situation was summed up for us by one of the teachers who attended the summer school we worked with in Belfast in July 1972. After three days of discussion in which he took little part, this teacher came to us and said: 'I've thought through what you've been saying about developing their language and I think you are right, but I don't know what to do. You see, I teach in a very formal school and I get order by a mixture of being tough and trying to be fair, but what you suggest means changing my whole way of going.'

This teacher could see the need, but he did not feel able to act at that moment. Subsequently he did act, and in spite of a very formal, indeed, rigid situation he did create a change in conditions within his own class-room. What he did in effect was to create what we might call a 'micro-climate', a small area within the general language-climate of the school where conditions were significantly different. Within the confines of his own room he was able to do something to off-set conditions in the school in general.

The pupils' view of change is crystallised for us by the group of fourth formers who, after about five weeks of the autumn term, got up a petition, demanding that the one of us concerned 'get on with teaching us something and stop all this talk'. The general climate of the school was not exactly supportive and most members of staff took a very 'subject content' view of their work. These fourth formers wanted work in English to conform to their expectations of what 'work' in a school context ought to look like. These expectations had no room for the idea that *they* had a positive contribution to make to their learning through their participation in various kinds of shared language activity.

What these two brief illustrations suggest is that the task of modifying the language climate of a school requires a concerted effort upon the part of the staff that may be very difficult to initiate. What they imply, however, is the degree to which any teacher could create for himself and his pupils a 'micro-climate' in the context of his own class-room. Whatever the nature of the language climate prevailing in a school, it is up to every teacher to decide for himself what he might do to modify its manifestations in so far as his own work is concerned.

Postscript

We ended our last chapter by suggesting that every teacher is in a position to consider how he could best enhance his pupils' ability to use the language they have in the context of the school, and to learn the language they need if they are to meet the school's demands in terms of language for learning, because every teacher has a local control over the linguistic micro-climate of his own classroom, however hostile to the linguistic needs of pupils the total climate of the school may be. Easily enough said, the reader may think, but how is it to be done? What kinds of things would create the conditions in the class-room that could lead to a favourable climate for language activity? How could these be reconciled with a prevailing climate that was hostile, or with the dictates of syllabus and public examination? Is it not the case, perhaps, that the curriculum of the secondary school, as we have it at present, creates the most hostile language climate of all for the large majority of secondary school pupils?

These questions are properly asked and point to the seriousness of the problems that face us if we wish to make use of our knowledge of language and community in order to develop a more effective approach to language as the medium of learning in the school context. Moreover, they imply that something major *can* be achieved by working to modify the habitual attitudes towards, and assumptions about, the use of language, both for living and for learning, that we customarily find in schools of all kinds at the present time. It may be in the minds of some readers that there is a body of recent research which has suggested the school counts for so little in relation to the combined weight of home and peer group that, really, nothing very much by way of change can be hoped for through changing the structure and practice of formal education. Throughout this book we have laid particular emphasis upon the critical interrelationship between language and community, in the sense that learning a language is the equivalent of learning a culture, and a culture is an expression for the whole body of values that go to make up a community. Surely, then, if school can do so little to modify the attitudes and assumptions pupils bring with them from their home and community, how likely is it that school will be able to modify the pupil's own language.

Again, this objection is a serious one. If it were true, then there would be little point in attempting more than a holding operation as far as the majority of pupils were concerned, and the relative temper of the language climate of the school would be a very minor matter. However, it seems to us that it is precisely the possibility of modifying pupils' ways of using language that gives the lie to this pessimistic view of the school's potential for change. We would see the language climate of the school as the critical factor in the school's ability to provide those alternative ways of seeing the world out of which changes in the pupils attitudes and assumptions might grow. It is this climate that determines whether or not he will be allowed to use the language he has learnt successfully as a social being in the new context of his formal education, and whether or not he will be given appropriate opportunities to learn the language he now needs, if he is to meet the demands of this formal education, in the only place where these needs can be provided for, *the context of the learning situations that give rise to them.* If the climate excludes from the school the pupil's own ways of using language, then it excludes also the pupil's own ways of looking at the world; and if it does not allow him to present his own ways of looking at the world, then it can scarcely expect to create the conditions in which the pupil might choose to modify them.

So this brings us back to the questions raised in the first paragraph of this Postscript and to the kinds of answers that would substantiate so strong a belief in the possibility of creating a favourable language climate for the school. Perhaps it is significant that the last paragraphs might read rather strangely to someone who works in the more progressive Infant or Junior school. At its best, the contemporary Infant school is an excellent example of how a language climate can be created that leads to continuous positive language learning. Another example is provided by the best work now being done in secondary schools by the English Departments that build their work around the pupil's exploration of his own experience through writing and talking about it in words of his own choosing. Another clue to the creation of a favourable language climate is provided by the approach Professor Stenhouse has developed for the Humanities Curriculum Project where, in effect, he requires the teacher, in the role of chairman, to create such a climate by himself remaining neutral. There is a similar requirement for the creation of a locally favourable climate implicit in the moral education material Peter McPhail has developed for Schools Council under the name of *Lifeline*.

These questions really require a rather different kind of answer, however, which would be directed specifically to the practical problems they raise. Part of this answer would be provided by a sequel to this book which would explore in detail the concept of language climate in the context of education, showing what features of the school situation and the interaction of the class-room are most significant in its formation, and how these affect pupils' and teachers' use of language for learning. This sequel we hope to be able to provide. That lies in the future, however. For the present, we can point to another part of the answer, the provision of practical help for the teacher who wants to try and do something about the language climate of his own class-room. Here he can turn to the resource for work with language called *Language in Use*, where he will find a wide range of suggestions about the ways in which class-room activities can be organised so as to give the maximum opportunities for pupils to develop their command of language, spoken and written.

Language in Use is so designed that the suggestions it offers can be adapted to the needs of any classroom, for it is a resource in the hands of the teacher, not a body of material for the pupil. Hence it is not limited in its application to any one age group or level of ability, nor need it be confined to any one area of the curriculum. It has by now been used in an enormous variety of individual learning situations, embracing as wide a range of language climates, from the most hostile to the most favourable. The cumulative experience of those who have used it suggest that the approaches recommended do succeed in creating a language climate, locally, in individual class-rooms, that enables pupils, *and their teachers*, to modify their ways of thinking about language and its use and, in the process, modify also their ways of using language. How and why this is possible is the subject of *Using 'Language in Use': a guide to language work in the class-room* by the present authors.

At this stage in the growth of our understanding of the part played by language in education, we need to develop our thinking along all three lines suggested by this Postscript. We need to know more about the processes by which we learn language, the effect of the context in which we first learn language upon our subsequent ways of using language, and upon our capacity to continue indefinitely the process of learning new ways of using language. We need to know much more about the inter-relationship between the language we use, the community we inhabit and the culture we express through the values we hold. We need to see much more clearly where the school fits into this complex pattern: how it regards pupils' existing capability as successful users of language for living; what demands it makes as a user of language for learning upon the individual's capacity to language, and to learn language; how it relates itself to the community from which it draws its pupils, and to the culture whose values their attitudes and assumptions embody. It is to meet such needs as these that *Explorations in Language Study* was established and *Language and Community* is one part of the process of demonstrating why these matters are so vitally important to everyone involved in education.

At the same time, we need to develop our ways of showing how such explorations as these can be related to day-to-day practice in class-rooms of all kinds with pupils of all ages and levels of ability. We must be able to offer some concrete guidance to the teacher who says, 'Yes, this makes good sense. I see where the old ways won't achieve what I want to achieve. What do I do about it?' We must show that new ideas can lead on into new practice, and that that new practice can then modify the ideas which gave rise to it, so that we can break down and discard, once and for all, the old bad distinction between Theory, the Province of those who wouldn't show how their ideas could work in practice, and Practice, the Province of those who wouldn't admit that ideas could have anything to do with their needs. Titles in the Series like Brian Harrison's *English as a Second and Foreign Language* and Eric Ashworth's *Language in the Junior School*, exemplify the necessary interrelationship between new ideas and new practice, while *Using 'Language in Use': a guide to language work in the class-room* is a detailed account of what a teacher can do to create a favourable language climate and how he can do it.

The third line along which our thinking must develop is a concrete realizing of our answers to the question, 'What do I do?', in terms of resources and materials. It is a sad reflection upon the educational scene that so many teachers are convinced that this is the *only* line that really matters. This view is epitomised by the teacher who rises to his feet after a presentation and says, 'That's all very well, but *what* do I do with 3g, second period on Monday next?', by which he means, regrettably, 'Give me something I can use and don't bother me with questions about the why's and wherefore's of using it.' This is really a plea for something to structure the time teacher and pupil spend together, irrespective of whether or not anything significant *happens* during that time. When we speak of 'resources and materials', we have in mind something very different, something that will enable the teacher to implement successfully the new practice he has decided upon, and not a means by which he can abdicate the responsibility for making decisions of that kind for himself. What we have in mind is exemplified by *Language in Use*, by *Lifeline*, by the Humanities Curriculum Project, where the resource requires the teacher to come to terms with new practice and think it through for himself before he can use it successfully. Each of these resources has great potential for helping a teacher to give concrete expression to his decision that the language climate in which he worked must change. They are not a substitute for that decision, however, and, in the absence of it, are likely to prove a sad disappointment.

We have come a long way from the point at which we began, with the new born infant, helpless and languageless, dependent for survival upon the supportive social context of family and community, and dependent upon the relationships of that human environment for the language without the learning of which survival will become difficult indeed. What we have tried to make plain in this Postscript is that the journey the reader has been asked to undertake does lead from that point right down to the discussion of resources and materials for use in the class-room, and that at no point along the way is it legitimate for him to make a break and say, 'Up to now it has all been very interesting, but this is where the nitty-gritty begins.' Ultimately, our every act in the class-room has to be seen against the broad design of how we use language to live and to learn, because that perspective alone will lead us to make the right choices in our day-to-day decisions, when those decisions involve language in the context of teaching and learning.

Notes on further reading

As the reader will imagine there is a vast literature lying behind the themes treated in this book, but we do not propose to shower him with titles, partly because we have a very realistic view of what it is possible for any one reader to find time for, and partly because we feel that lengthy bibliographies are valuable only to those who are already reasonably familiar with the literature of the fields concerned and we have written specifically for those to whom these fields are very new. Full references follow at the end of this section.

Let us begin, therefore, by listing the books which have contributed directly to the thinking that has gone into this book. *An Introduction to the Study of Man* is a very large book, but it has an excellently detailed table of contents, so that anyone who wanted to follow up the ideas we have drawn from it would find it very easy to do so. *Inquiring Man* is the most accessible way of finding out more about the ideas of George Kelly, but it is not an easy book to read, for the ideas it discusses are complex and the writing is very compressed. The most accessible way of finding out more about the social aspects of our argument is to turn to *Language and Social Behaviour*, where again the reader is helped in his search by a very detailed table of contents. Chapter 8, 'Social class and language' and Chapter 9 'Social class, language and socialisation' are particularly relevant to the argument of the book. Chapter 8 contains the most lucid account of Bernstein's work available, but the reader who wants to tackle Bernstein for himself can best do so by turning to *Class, Codes and Control*, and begin by reading Bernstein's own Introduction. He should then read Paper 9, 'Social class, language and socialisation'.

For the view of language we have used, *Exploring Language* provides a first step, especially Chapter 7, 'Command of a language', while Chapters 5 and 6, 'Language and relationships', and 'Language and society' have more to say about our view of how we use language to live. The reader can then turn to the work of M. A. K. Halliday, starting with two papers in *Explorations in the Functions of Language*, 'Relevant models of language' and 'Language in a social perspective'. He should then try 'Learning how to mean', in his volume of the same name.

It is less easy to point to any one source for our thinking about community, though we must say that the situation in Northern Ireland over the last five years has provided a shaping context for it. We have learnt much from the sort of work summarised so ably in *Communities in Britain*, and from original studies of particular human environments such as *Akenfield*, *The Classic Slum* and *The Unprivileged*. Beyond that lies the more formal literature of social science, where we would point to the work of Erving Goffman, especially *The Presentation of Self in Everyday Life*, a highly readable and entertaining book, and Peter Berger, whose work on the concept of social reality is crucial to our thinking. It has to be said, however, that this is formidable territory to enter for the reader who is not familiar with the language of sociological theory.

From the ever-growing literature about pupils, schools and their relationships, we would mention three titles only, each one of which explores from its own position many of the ideas we approach from our linguistic perspective, *Society, Schools and Humanity; Young Teachers and Reluctant Learners* and *Teaching as a Subversive Activity*. The vast bulk of the literature of educational studies is arid indeed, but each of these books is pungent, readable and sharply focused on the needs of pupils and their problems.

Finally, there is the professional aspect of all that we have said in this book, the implication that every teacher, and everyone else who is concerned directly with schools and education, ought to come to terms with what we can now say about the part played by language in education. The first two chapters of *Exploring Language* offer a brief consideration of what is involved, but the reader will find the fully developed argument which underlies the aim of this present book set out in Part I of *Language Study, the Teacher and the Learner*, 'The concept of language study'. Part II of that book, 'A Guide to Reading in Language Study' is there for the reader who is now ready to make his own way into the literature and find out for himself what the exploration of language in education might have to offer him.

An Introduction to the Study of Man, J. Z. Young. Oxford 1971.
Inquiring Man: the Theory of Personal Constructs, D. Bannister and Fay Fransella. Penguin 1971.
Language and Social Behaviour, W. P. Robinson. Penguin 1972.
Class, Codes and Control Vol. I, Basil Bernstein. Routledge and Kegan Paul 1971, and Paladin 1973.
Exploring Language, Peter Doughty, John Pearce and Geoffrey Thornton. Edward Arnold 1972.
Explorations in the Functions of Language, M. A. K. Halliday. Edward Arnold 1973.
Learning How to Mean: Explorations in the Development of Language, M. A. K. Halliday. Edward Arnold 1974.
Communities in Britain, Ronald Frankenberg. Pelican 1966.
Akenfield, Ronald Blythe. Penguin 1972.
The Classic Slum, Robert Roberts. Pelican 1973.
The Unprivileged, Jeremy Seabrook. Longmans Green 1967 and Penguin 1973.
The Presentation of Self in Everyday Life, Erving Goffman. Allen Lane The Penguin Press 1969.
The Social Construction of Reality, Peter Berger and Thomas Luckmann. Allen Lane The Penguin Press 1967 and Penguin University Books 1971.
Society, Schools and Humanity, Douglas Holly. Paladin 1971.
Young Teachers and Reluctant Learners, Charles Hannam, Pat Smyth and Norman Stephenson. Penguin 1971.
Teaching as a Subversive Activity, Neil Postman and Charles Weingartner. Penguin 1971.
Language Study, the Teacher and the Learner, Peter Doughty and Geoffrey Thornton. Edward Arnold 1973.

Resources and materials referred to in the Postcript

Language in Use, Peter Doughty, John Pearce and Geoffrey Thornton. Edward Arnold 1971.
Using 'Language in Use', a teacher's guide to language work in the classroom, Anne and Peter Doughty. Edward Arnold.
Humanities Curriculum Project. Heinemann.
Lifeline. Longman.